PRAISE FOR SUGAR HIGH

"JUST BRILLIANT. AN ABSOLUTE PAGE TURNER, WRITTEN
IN ALEX'S INIMITABLE VOICE, AND BRIMMING OVER WITH
ENTERTAINING ADVENTURES FROM THE FILM INDUSTRY AND
HER QUEST FOR KNOWLEDGE OF THIS COMMONLY
MISUNDERSTOOD HEALTH CONDITION."

- ELIZABETH HURLEY, ACTRESS & ENTREPRENEUR

"*SUGAR HIGH* IS AN ADDICTING AND ENGAGING
MASHUP OF A CELEBRITY MEMOIR AND AN INFORMATIVE
STORY THAT MILLIONS SHARE."

- EMILY LONGERETTA, US WEEKLY

"*SUGAR HIGH* IS SPECTACULAR. A SUPERB WAY FOR PEOPLE
TO GAIN AN UNDERSTANDING ABOUT DIABETES IN AN
ALLURING AND EXCITING WAY."

- ANNE PETERS, MD
PROFESSOR OF MEDICINE, USC. DIRECTOR OF THE
USC CLINICAL DIABETES PROGRAMS

D1489652

SUGAR HiGH

The Unexpected Journey of an
Inexperienced Type 1 Diabetic

Written by
Alexandra Park

RBL PUBLISHING

Discover more books from **RBL PUBLISHING**:

A MERMAID'S GUIDE:
EMPOWER YOUR CHILD IN WATER AND IN LIFE
Create safe, joyful swimmers starting in the bathtub.

WHERE THE SANITY ENDS
A humorous parody of "Where the Sidewalk Ends" for parents.

- DEDICATION -

To my Mum, who has championed my every move
and stood by my side at the face of every hurdle.

To anyone who's facing a challenge on their way
to becoming who they want to be.

10% OF AUTHOR ROYALTIES ARE DONATED TO DIABETES-RELATED NOT-FOR-PROFITS,
INCLUDING *LIFE FOR A CHILD*.

•v•

Sugar High by Alexandra Park

© 2021 Alexandra Park
Published by RBL Publishing, a division of RBL Studios Inc.

NOTE FROM THE AUTHOR:
To anyone with new onset T1D, it's important for me to point out that hypoglycemia/lows don't have to be as frequent or life-impacting as they once were. The field of diabetes has been advancing quickly in terms of technology and my story is not a reflection or indication of what needs to happen to all people with type 1 diabetes.

For permissions contact:
SugarHighBook@gmail.com

Edited by Joe Greathead
Line Editing by Adele O. Kuforiji
Headshot Photography by Aaron Barry
Cover Design by Semnitz (semnitz@gmail.com)
Produced by Michelle Lang

ISBN: 978-1-951756-01-7 (pb)
ISBN: 978-1-951756-02-4 (hc)
Ebook ISBN: 978-1-951756-03-1

www.RBLStudios.org

First Edition
Printed in the U.S.A.

- TABLE OF CONTENTS -

-SPECIAL THANKS-

James Lafferty, Michelle Lang,
Pip Greathead, Joe Greathead, Dr. Anne Peters,
Elizabeth Hurley, Mark Greathead, Benedicte Herlihy,
Ngoc Nguyen, Aaron Barry, Michaela Trott,
and Tom Austen.

A NOTE FROM THE AUTHOR:

Sugar High is about a time in my life when two very unrelated but equally momentous things happened at once.   I was one of those very lucky people who landed on earth knowing exactly what I wanted to be when I grew up, an actor. After 10 or so years of fairly consistent rejection, albeit a - some might say - commendable hustle, I booked myself a one way ticket to Hollywood to search for what I wasn't finding at home in Australia. Three months before I was set to leave for Los Angeles, I was diagnosed with type 1 diabetes. With five grand in the bank, a tourist visa and a very foggy comprehension of type 1 diabetes, I went anyway. Ten days after arriving, I was cast as a lead character in a big American TV show, *The Royals*.

Sugar High spans five years from the time I was diagnosed and takes the reader all over the world: Sydney, Los Angeles, New York, London, Paris, Cannes, Amalfi and Mexico. The story flickers notes of the aspirational celebrity/living-the-dream theme, while simultaneously exploring the struggle of an inexperienced type 1 diabetic. It's educational, in a way, but only in that the reader will be learning what I learned, as I learned it. At its heart, *Sugar High* is about a journey to acceptance, learning to let go of the illusion of perfection and searching for humor even in the darkest moments. Most of all, it's about reminding yourself to enjoy the ride.

I wrote this book because I want to help people like me, for the children and young adults who were hit by the same meteorite and still have dreams. I want them to know those dreams are still possible and that, oftentimes, the true magic tends to come after a bit of a mess. At the end of the day, I just wanted to write a book about diabetes that entertains and inspires, one that I wished for, but failed to find when I embarked upon my own journey.

If I've achieved what I set out to do, the reader should feel both a sense of peace and a wave of excitement to have found a friend in this book. This is not a sob story, nor a humorless lecture. This is a meditation on dusting yourself off and trying again. Keeping those dreams at the front and center regardless of whatever shit's been thrown in your face. It's funny and a little frightening at times - but mostly funny - and also empowering.

Sugar High is told in my voice, slightly rough around the edges, a little emotional at times, pretty whacky most of the time and intentionally imperfect.

It's a lot like life itself.

1

PEEING IN THE DARK

It was one of those moments, like in the movies, when the movement and laughter of a party fade out of focus, and the camera zooms in on the lead character smiling contentedly with a glass of wine in her hand. A single, happy tear escaping before being swiftly wiped away. It was my 23rd birthday and I'd organized a "grown-up dinner" to celebrate. I sat there, drinking my third glass of bulk brought, "bring your own" vino, seated at the head of an extendable picnic table the local pizza joint had arranged especially for me. At that moment, I felt an overwhelming rush of invincibility. A tantalizing realization that everything was going according to the plan and, more than that, like anything could happen.

I'd recently flown the nest and moved into an apartment in Freshwater on the northern beaches of Sydney, with my boyfriend. Luke was a charismatic pro surfer who I "coincidentally" met the year prior, while visiting my best friend Tarah, who was working in France. I say "coincidentally" in inverted commas because our meeting wasn't a coincidence at all. It was more like flat out stalking. Tarah used to date one of Luke's surfing buddies who happened to be in France at the same time she was, along with the rest of the Australian National team. I was desperate to see my best mate, had saved up enough money for the plane ticket, and was feeling romantically optimistic. Let's face it, the surf team sounded a bit like something I needed to see for myself. After creepily sifting through the list of blonde babes she'd emailed through, as a clever and final persuasion tactic, I landed on Luke and a tiny little dove flew out of my chest. I jumped on the next plane to France and, once there, basically kept "bumping into him" until he agreed to go out with me. So, here we were, months later and already adulting to the finest degree, shacked up with our best mates Tarah and Brett in a seaside hamlet, sharing all the love we had to offer between us. I mean sometimes things just fucking work out, don't they?

The other fantastic thing that had me feeling light as a feather, and free as a bird, was that I'd just received word that I'd finally booked a real acting gig. It wasn't the lead in a Baz Lurhman film, but it was something, and something was everything when it came to the hustle of a long time struggling actor. I'd won the role of Robyn, an emotionally deranged hippie, on the long running Australian soap opera *Home and Away*. This is actually not the first time I've played a fleeting character on *Home and Away*. I did a few episodes back when I was 19. Australia is huge but has a very small television industry, so it's not uncommon for actors to play different characters on the same show.

Anyway, the role was just for a few episodes, meaning by no means would you find my face on the poster, nor did it mean I'd quite arrived at the "quit the day job" stage just yet. A proper acting job, regardless of its shelf life, was something that didn't happen often, and it was everything I had been working towards. I'd been given the opportunity to do the thing I loved most in the world, on an actual set. It felt like winning the lottery. Just to be there, to be a part of it, surrounded by the magic of it all made it feel like my dream was possible. It was a highly welcomed sign that I had to be on the right track.

So, post-birthday celebration, my first few weeks as a 23-year-old were spent zipping the length of Sydney from the *Home and Away* set and back to the cash register, where I worked as a sales assistant in a swanky women's clothing store. Adrenaline was running hot. I'd taken a monumental step closer to my lifelong dream of becoming an actor. I had secured a sexy athletic boyfriend, had a handful of bucks in the bank, an independent living space and what felt like my whole life ahead of me. The adrenaline was coming from multiple directions and it was powerful, so powerful that it prevented me from feeling what my body had recently been trying to tell me.

One morning, we were scheduled to film on location in Palm Beach, a picturesque, upscale community further up Sydney's northern beaches. I jumped in the car in a huff, excited for the day ahead, and spent the 30 minute coastal drive racking my brain for an explanation as to why I'd just had another big, upsetting fight with Luke. I couldn't seem to rationalize how it started, or how it got so bad, other than a slight inkling that he wasn't to blame.

I'd arrived about 40 minutes before my call time, parked my Mazda 3 on the shoreline, ran across the road for another much needed coffee, downed it in two sips, then returned to my car to compile an apology text to Luke. I had mood swings lately, they were coming out of nowhere and starting to take an unwelcome toll on our otherwise idyllic home life. So there I sat, texting away, listening to the sound of waves crashing, overlooking my actual dream come true: a film crew bustling about with equipment against the backdrop of a sun still low and pink, rising over the ocean. It was one of those gorgeous days I'd always longed for, but for some strange and unidentifiable reason, the feeling enveloping me was warped. It was like a deep swirling black hole of fear and general yuck.

With 10 minutes to spare before the day's work started, I flipped down the visor for a quick reflection check. Mortified. Bags for days, like I'd just been punched in both eyes. A confronting image of utmost exhaustion for which I had to assume my recent wacky sleeping patterns were to blame. Peeing 5-8 times a night was another new development I'd been sweeping under the rug. I figured it was just a phase that was becoming slightly alarming and infuriating. After reminding myself that makeup can cover just about anything, I focused on some breathing exercises and attempted to get my shit together.

In the makeup trailer, I attempted ample small talk with the makeup artist, who appeared politely, yet noticeably frustrated by the deep cystic acne that had gotten inexplicably worse since the last time I saw her. I could have counted on one hand how many pimples I'd had before turning 23. Lately it felt like some kind of payback was being served for all those years of spotless teenage bliss, like a delayed stretch of puberty.

I was scrolling through pictures of puppies on my phone, grateful for the buzz of hairdryers and conversations that didn't require my participation. While reminding myself of the meaning of life, I overheard one of the girls asking for a tampon. "A tampon!" I thought. It felt like a lightbulb had been switched on. Hopeful and desperate that perhaps my own cycle was to blame for the recent struggles, I whipped out the calendar app. I counted the days back to my last period three times before defeatedly heading back to the album of puppies. I'd have to look elsewhere for answers.

I'd only been in a hair and makeup trailer a handful of times before that gig, but enjoyed each one of them beyond words. It felt like warming up for some championship game you'd been dying to play, the one you'd been working towards your whole life (I'd imagine, never having been quite the championship-calibre athlete myself). The energy was contagious, uplifting, exhilarating and all of this was the opposite of what I was feeling that day. There was all this magic going on around me, but it felt just out of reach, like I wasn't supposed to be there or something shitty like that. While thanking the girls for the stellar aesthetic improvement, I made an excuse for my glassy eyes, mentioned the pollen had been giving me trouble lately, and headed to the breakfast line.

After an embarrassingly large plate of breakfast, I felt empty and utterly unnourished. This was another recurring theme, since turning 23, that I appreciated least of all on days when I was filming and really counting on food to do its job and fuel my brain for a big day on set. I walked down to the shoreline, costumed up in an elaborate gypsy-type ensemble, and started to feel more nervous than excited. That was far from normal considering I was walking towards the thing that excited me more than anything: a group of people holding booms and camera equipment, gearing up for a scene. I truly lived for those days on set. I should have been in my element, but everything just... felt... off.

Somewhat serendipitously, the scene we were shooting that morning was one that established my character in a state of intense sadness and disillusion. I reasoned this was a silver lining, as at least I'd arrived emotionally on point. Tears on tap baby, that's one thing I had going for me. Once the cameras started rolling, it was easier to push the fear of whatever the hell was going on with me aside. Regardless of how internally shitty I felt, my only wish was that the day would never end. Whether I was on a set, being intensely yelled at by my acting teacher, or delivering lines to my own reflection sitting cross-legged on the bedroom floor, acting always made me feel better. Even the arduous, two year audition process for drama school was utterly invigorating. Even after being rejected twice in a row. So, as per usual, I walked off the set that day feeling a hell of a lot better than I did that morning. The pep was truly back in my step, so much so that I'd basically forgotten all of the morning's dramatic concerns and put it all down to my occasional tendency to dramatize.

While driving back to Freshwater, AKA "the love nest," I felt like myself again and I couldn't wait to get home and reassure Luke that he hadn't made a mistake in agreeing to move in with me. I thought that arriving home with a delicious dinner might accelerate the process and called in an order from our favorite Italian restaurant which, conveniently, happened to be on the way home.

After a solid 15 minutes of feel-good tunes to accompany the rebirth of my spirit, I pulled up to the intersection that I could have sworn turned onto Morris Street AKA "the pizza street," but was having a hard time making out the letters on the street sign. I leaned forward and squinted like an 85 year old woman. I wiped my eyes, and blinked a few times but the letters were all still blurry. I was frozen at the light for a brief "Am I having a stroke?" panic, then startled by an obnoxious honk from the car behind me. Flustered, I put my foot on the gas before I had time to check if it was safe to go, only to notice a pedestrian making his way onto the crosswalk. He saw me coming, thank God, and jumped back onto the curb, but I'd never been more rattled in my life. I could have hit him. After hastily pulling the car to the side of the road, I raced over to the gentleman to apologize and made sure he was OK. Then I got back in the car and tried to calm myself down before resuming my search for the pizza street. After slowly rounding the block a couple of times, I was convinced that my momentary lapse in vision wasn't so momentary at all. It wasn't dark out, there was nothing in my eyes, and yet it seemed that pretty much anything out of close range looked strangely out of focus.

Since turning 23, I'd been to the medical center twice to address these mounting symptoms, for peace of mind more than anything. I left both times with the diagnosis that I was absolutely fine, which, sure enough, was what I wanted to hear and therefore tried to believe. I managed to push the physical discomfort aside, but was still struggling to filter the dueling voices in my head. That afternoon was a turning point though. I could no longer hear the voice that said everything was fine. All I could hear was the voice that said something was terribly wrong. I started to feel panicked that my sudden impaired eyesight had come as a result of ignoring all the previous warning signs. A sense of dread set in when I considered that, left unchecked, whatever was ailing me could have disastrous consequences. Up to this point, I'd reasoned that the perpetual exhaustion was a result of my strange sleeping patterns. The anxiety and mood swings must have emerged from the fatigue. The weight loss didn't really bother me and the acne I'd figured was just a stage. The constant demand for food and water hadn't really worried me either, but almost hitting someone with my car did. That's for fucking certain. I started to feel like I was going mad.

After driving home via voice prompts, about 20km (about 12 miles) under the speed limit, Luke and I talked everything over. We decided that regardless of how badly I'd hoped what the doctors had said was true, I was really not, in fact, "fine".

2

A SLAP IN THE FACE WITH A COLD, WET, FISH.

It would have been brilliant to leave the medical center the following morning with a definitive diagnosis and prescription for something that would get rid of the nasty symptoms I had been experiencing.

Instead, I left with the same "you're likely just a bit run down," a pat on the back and minus sixty bucks.

On the drive home, I called my Mum, otherwise known as Pippy G. Prior to that afternoon, I hadn't been completely transparent with her regarding my physical health. I relayed to her that I'd just left my third doctor's appointment in three weeks but that everything seemed to check out, and I'd hopefully be feeling better soon. My Mum is a renowned speech pathologist and has worked in the hospital system for over 40 years, so she knows a thing or two about the unfortunate reality that doctors don't always get it right. While bringing her up to speed on the symptoms, I heard movement and the rattling of keys on the other end of the line. By the time I got to the part about how long they'd been around, I heard a door slam. While walking her through the three trips to the local medical center, I heard the phone switch from handheld to bluetooth. After telling her what all three doctors had said, I heard the rev of an engine and some pretty rude words. As much as I wanted answers, the quick dismissal from doctor number three had provided a sort of numbing sense of hope. Mum wasn't having any of it though, and was idling out front in her Corolla by the time I got home.

I appreciated Mum's benevolent attempt to distract me from the anxiety that accompanied our mad rush over to Anita, our family doctor. Her driving style was a bit mental. Mum dabbled with the idea of becoming a race car driver before she found speech pathology. My siblings and I are reminded of that fact whenever she's revved up. Mum kept forgetting where she was mid-sentence, but regardless of her contagious concern, I believed her when she said everything was going to be OK.

While seated in the familiar consulting room, holding Mum's hand tight like a vice, Dr. Anita smiled kindly and asked me to start by telling her what was going on. While I appreciated Dr. Anita's maternal vibe, her laser focused kindness made me feel significantly more freaked out than the previous doctors and their flat-out bored, half-asleep demeanor. While taking a crack at answering Dr. Anita's questions, I fought the intense urge to bawl my eyes out, but failed miserably. She handed me a tissue, leaned in closer and told me to take my time. Via snotty, sputtered English, I listed off the symptoms as best I could while Dr. Anita gently nodded along. It was almost as though the moment I managed to get one out, she knew what the next one would be. She was listening intently, doing the math as I gave her the numbers, and it seemed as if it was all adding up to something she'd seen before. With kind consideration, Dr. Anita gave very little away as I finished my ramble, but said she wanted to take blood immediately.

The next morning was intense. Sleepy Mum rolled over, flipped her phone the right way up and almost fell out of bed, shocked by 12 missed calls from pathology and Dr. Anita's office. There was a knock at the door. It was only 7:00 a.m. and the knock was persistent, which told her it couldn't have been Amazon or Vera from next door returning mail that went in the wrong box. Mum threw on her Ugg boots and fluffy robe and answered the door to another half asleep, yet very concerned mother, also dressed in Ugg boots and a robe. Dr. Anita had slammed her vehicle into park across the driveway, apologized profusely for the alarming, unfortunately necessary visit and went on to tell Mum the not-so-good news. She said that as a matter of urgency, Mum should get me to a hospital as soon as possible. I had a blood glucose reading of 41.3 mmol/L (744.1 mg/dl), which is about eight times higher than what it should have been, and there was a good chance I had developed type 1 diabetes.

Back at the love shack in Freshwater, happily dead to the world, I was awoken by drips of salty water and cold hands. It was Luke holding his cellphone, "Alex, you gotta wake up. Your Mum is on the phone." After failing to get through to me, Mum had managed to catch Luke on his way back from a surf. Luke knew better than to wake the beast (me) on a normal day, let alone during those times when I was up all night peeing. I had to assume it was something important, possibly regarding the gallon of blood that was drained out of my arm the previous day. He handed me the phone with an expression that was hard to read.

Standing in my undies with the phone on loudspeaker, I opened the curtains, waited for my system to boot up, and attempted to keep up with what sounded like a one-way voice message from a woman with a hell of a lot to say and very little time to say it. While only registering about 23% of what the very flustered Pippy G was saying, I managed to catch the words "type 1 diabetes," which meant nothing to me at the time, other than having to assume it was something I might have. Before there was time for any follow-up questions on my end, Pippy G told me to stay put and keep my ringer on before hanging up to take a call from her brother, my Uncle Jim, who I vaguely recalled might have had diabetes. Obeying Mum's orders like the good little girl I strive to be, I sat on the end of the bed and stared directly into the mirror with no particular feelings at all, heart rate of 60 to 100. I was truly just, sitting.

While looking in the mirror, I was distracted by an enchanting Rainbow Lorikeet that had made its way onto the balcony. It wandered close enough to be almost inside and just stood there, entirely still, staring at me through the mirror. I stared right back, examining the breathtaking colors of its feathers. I could tell you with 89% certainty that at that moment, the Lorikeet and I were gazing deeply into each other's souls. We were complete strangers, but it felt like that bird had my back and I had no reason to believe otherwise.

Breaking what felt like an intensely intimate moment with the Lorikeet, my thigh began to vibrate, it was Pippy G again. Uncle Jim had put her in contact with his endocrinologist friend, Dr. Susan. Despite Dr. Anita's recommendation, Dr. Susan told my Mum not to take me to the hospital, claiming it was potentially traumatic, but rather to come in and see her right away. Apparently, I needed something called insulin that they could administer immediately.

Insulin and endocrinologist were both words I had likely overheard twice in my life prior to that moment, but words that Pippy G assured me would be explained once we got to Uncle Jim's friend, the endocrinologist. She was already on her way to pick me up.

I had to assume that - yet again - Pippy G didn't abide by the speed limit on her journey across town. Before I had time to identify an appropriate pair of pants she dragged me from my apartment and prodded me into her Corolla. Within the next five minutes we were climbing the stairs to the office space above my local Thai restaurant, if you can believe it. Not once, while waiting for my Pad See Ew, did I ever ponder what might happen in the offices above.

I sat in the unfussy waiting room, flipped through a sticky old gossip mag from 2003, and felt unusually calm. Delectable garlic-infused aromas wafted through the window from downstairs, and Pippy G seemed relatively chill as well. I still hadn't fully registered the words "type 1 diabetes." They were up there, floating around in the ether, but I suppose you could say I wasn't jumping to conclusions just yet.

With an invincibility coat draped firmly over my shoulders, I followed Mum into the doctor's office where we were introduced to Dr. Susan. Dr. Susan might have been the tallest woman I had ever seen in my life! She had blonde hair and wore fairly disappointing sandals that exposed her equally discouraging toes (though I'm not sure how important that is right now). While Dr. Susan completed her pleasantries, I sat in a small, old chair by the window and noticed a couple of my friends parking their car, gathering their surfboards and heading down to the beach for a day of normal, 23 year-old life.

Pippy G and I sat there in silence, holding hands, as Dr. Sue flipped through some papers and introduced us to a lady called Elma, who smelt a bit like chicken, but not in a bad way. According to Dr. Sue, Elma was to be my diabetes educator, which felt a bit like we were jumping the gun. I wondered if perhaps we might start with an explanation and confirmation before we got to the education.

The ladies were fussing quite a bit, which was starting to test my overall serenity and provoked me to jump in and ask if either Elma or Dr. Sue would confirm whether or not I, in fact, *had* type 1 diabetes or if this was still something we were trying to figure out. Dr. Sue had a matronly vibe and replied sternly, saying that there was no doubt in her mind that with a blood glucose reading of 41.3 mmol/L (744.1 mg/dl)[1], not only did I definitely have type 1 diabetes, I was lucky to be alive. She said that I was lucky to have found it as quickly as I did without causing life long damage.

After catching on to Dr. Sue's rather blunt bedside manner, I was feeling a little pissed off and decided to take the reins on the session with some additional questions that I was fairly keen for somebody to answer. I started by asking if she would kindly explain to me exactly what type 1 diabetes was. Elma chimed in and said type 1 diabetes is a chronic condition in which the pancreas produces little or no insulin, and that insulin is the hormone needed to allow glucose to enter the cells to

---

1   The international standard for measuring blood glucose levels is by 'molar concentration,' measured in mmol/L (millimoles per litre; or millimolar) - which is what we use in Australia. However, In the United States, where they use imperial measurements for everything else except this, it is measured in mg/dl (milligrams per decilitre). The readings mean the same thing; there's just two ways to understand them. For the purpose of this book, I'll show you both, like this: 4 (72) , where 4 is the Australian measurement, and 72 is the American equivalent.

produce energy. As appreciative as I was for the succinct response, I told Elma that, though it may come as a surprise to her, I was going to need her to explain this shit like she was explaining it to someone who's never had reason or desire to know what insulin or pancreas or any other words like those meant. Dr. Sue took over again, and after stopping her after each sentence for clarification, I began to understand. She said type 1 diabetes is an autoimmune disease, a condition where your immune system mistakenly attacks your body. In this case, my immune system had attacked the insulin-producing cells in my pancreas, causing them to cease production. In people without diabetes, the pancreas produces the exact amount of insulin required to break down whatever food has been eaten and sends glucose to the kidneys, liver, and muscles, creating energy that functions the body. Without insulin, the body is unable to break down glucose. This means the food you eat has no way of getting to where it needs to go, leaving you depleted of energy, putting your body into a starvation state. I asked her to explain what the high number meant, the number that was eight times higher than what it should have been. She explained that in addition to transporting glucose where it needs to go, insulin is responsible for regulating the concentrated glucose that is forever present in the human bloodstream. The normal amount of glucose in the bloodstream is between 4mmol/L and 6mmol/L (72mg/dl - 108mg/dl). Without insulin, glucose cannot enter cells and instead builds up in the bloodstream. If left untreated, it sends the body into a state of hyperglycemia, which can lead to a diabetic coma or even death.

So what I took from all that was: my pancreas had corked it. The food I ate essentially went straight through me and autoimmune meant it wasn't my fault. We hadn't gotten to what caused it or how long I'd had it. Dr. Sue didn't have an answer for the cause, but went on to say that stress could have been a trigger. She asked me if I underwent any kind of physical or mental stress at the beginning of the year that might have provoked my body to react in this way. "Stress," I thought. For fuck's sake.

I'll be upfront and admit that I'd rarely been referred to as a yogi. I suppose I was a slightly intense person, but wouldn't have gone so far to identify myself as a palpable stress head. With a raised eyebrow and a slightly squinted eye, Pippy G indicated that she remembered some stress from six months ago. Oh yeah, six months ago I was over in Los Angeles participating in a hellish, cattle-call-type event known as pilot season where thousands of actors from all over the world congregate in Hollywood for a six week marathon of auditions for potential new TV shows.

I spent a typical day during pilot season manically driving around the city, plowing as best I could through back-to-back auditions where I'd only had about five minutes to prepare. When I wasn't in the car or being shoved out the door by a casting director saying "Don't call us, we'll call you," I was usually crying into a bowl of Trader Joe's muesli and praying to Jehovah for just the slightest crumb of encouragement from my agent. I didn't book a role in the end, hardly anyone ever does, and, yes, it was an incredibly stressful experience. I now had to assume it was at least partly responsible for my broken pancreas. "Follow your dreams," they said.

Dr. Sue didn't specifically confirm that the attempt to follow my dreams was the culprit, but she did explain that both genetics and environmental factors appear to play a role in the process. I was starting to feel like I'd had enough. Not only was I receiving confirmation that something pretty serious was wrong with me, but I was also hearing that the thing I planned on doing for the rest of my life was likely what caused it.

Unfortunately, the ladies weren't quite done. It was then time for Elma to get on with her diabetes "educating," which naturally had me sitting on the edge of my seat. Elma started by walking me through the injection procedure, while telling me that nothing in my life needed to change. She advised that I should just carry on living my life as I had been. The only difference would be that from now on, I would have to inject the insulin that was no longer being produced on its own. So, yes, no changes at all. Next, she placed an insulin pen beside what looked like a toddlers drawing of a bowl of cornflakes, demonstrating - as if to a three-year-old - that I was to take a shot (pointed at the pen) before every meal (pointed at the drawing). Every fucking meal. I could tell Elma was trying to be helpful, but her uplifting, happy-go-lucky attitude felt increasingly patronizing by that point. I started to feel a bit sweaty and panicky as Elma kindly told me that as soon as I started taking the insulin I'd likely gain quite a bit of weight! Could have done without that tidbit, thanks babe!

But wait, there was more.

In order to figure out what my blood sugar was, and, therefore, how much insulin to inject, I was to use a glamorous device known as a glucose monitor. It was a little handheld device and Elma yanked my index finger to the bottom of it. She pressed a button that shot out something fucking sharp and pointy, resulting in a pea-sized drop of blood that I was to place on a test strip.

Pippy G was taking notes feverishly. I started to cry. Elma then explained that I could also, if I wanted, use a wearable device for delivering insulin and reading blood glucose. She ceremoniously unveiled a mortifying strap-on, rubber-stomach-replica that was covered with medical devices, about four or five of them. To my virginal eye, the crowding devices hanging off the rubber tum looked like mini-remote controls or children's building blocks, all meshed together and connected to plastic tubes and wires. It looked like something out of *Prometheus*. I'd had enough, bawling my fucking eyes out and heart racing like a packhorse. All I wanted to do was throw the stupid thing out the window and then cry until I died.

I told Pippy G there was absolutely no way in hell I would wear any of those things. I wasn't down for being connected to tubes. It felt like the session had been going on for a week, like a form of just-bearable torture. I got up from my seat, asked Elma to just give me the manual option and load me up with the bits so I could get the fuck out of there. The information went in one ear and out the other by that point anyway.

While making pace for the exit, Elma offered me some pamphlets with pictures of "happy, healthy fellow type 1's," all of whom were smiling creepily, wearing their remote controls on their abdomens, chords hanging out all over the place. It was as though they were speaking to me without words, saying "Come join us, you'll wear a computer on your stomach that everyone can see. You'll put on weight and we can all be friends!" It was too much - way too much and way too soon. My mind started doing backflips. I imagined myself at the beach, wearing the device. How do I even go swimming? How do I exercise? How do I wear clothes? How do I fit into the only world I've known with all this horrible shit you're telling me I need to do in order to stay alive?!

I told Elma to hold on to her pamphlets, grabbed Pippy by the sleeve of her sweater, and ran out the door.

3

THE SHOW MUST GO ON &
AN ELEPHANT NAMED ELLIS

After escaping the doctor's office, Mum and I sat at a side alley cafe for a post-apocalyptic latte. We said very little. I opened a packet of sugar, poured the contents onto the table and crushed the granules with a spoon. As I rolled and crunched, Mum stirred her latte with purpose and vigor, like she was born to stir that fucker. We sat there speaking without words for what felt like 25 minutes or so. We stirred and crunched in silent harmony, mutually relieved to be anywhere but the sobering clinic upstairs with its bad news B-S.

Breaking the silence and with some foam on her nose, Pippy G asked me what I wanted to do for the rest of the day. She wasn't aware that I was due on set in a couple of hours for my last scene on *Home and Away*. Until that moment I'd actually forgotten too, but noticed the cloud above my head morph from a dark grey to a light fluffy blue once I remembered. "I've gotta head to the studios in a bit," I said with a smile that was met with a look of concern. Mum was actively troubled by my eagerness to immediately return to work and protested for obvious reasons. All the while, she knew full well that it would take a lot more than what happened that morning to keep me away from the set.

Before hitting the gas in the Mazda, I decided to leave the events of the morning in Freshwater tightly sealed in a box to be dealt with later. I hadn't the fuzziest as to when I'd be graced with another opportunity to do the thing I loved most and firmly believed I was born to do. As far as I knew, the scene that afternoon could have been it for a while and therefore I intended to enjoy every second of the one I had left.

I figured a power ballad to accompany the drive was a profound first step. I went with "Rainy Days on Mondays" by The Carpenters, as it had never failed to make me feel inspired, emotive, and often flat-out invincible. With the windows down and the volume thunderous, I redirected the emerging dark thoughts and flatted them with what I believed to be realistic positivity. I reasoned that it could always be worse. Allegedly I had type 1 diabetes, but it wasn't cancer. It wasn't going to be as straightforward and simple as taking a pill every morning, but as Elma shrewdly pointed out, I would still be able to do everything I normally did. Above all, I was on my way to do some acting. The way I decided to see it, setbacks were and would always be inevitable. They were things I'd been conditioned to deal with in my experience as a struggling actor. Knockbacks, rejection, road blocks, curveballs, they're a pain in the ass, but all you have to do is find a way around them, over them, and under them. You figure it out. I knew everything was going to be fine and planned on using the hiccup as fuel to the fire.

In the few hours I spent at the studio that day, I was sort of shifting between two rather conflicting head spaces. On one hand, I felt like a bit of champ and even flirted with the idea that this diabetes thing could potentially add to my desired edgy appeal. On the other hand, I felt a spooky sort of numbness mixed with shock and disbelief. I don't think I fully believed what had just happened. Maybe part of me felt like I was going to get a call from the doctor telling me they'd gotten it wrong. I guess part of me felt like maybe it could be temporary. In any case, the magic that always came with being on set allowed me to keep my head in the game and in those few hours, I managed to almost completely forget about it .

Once I'd left the studios, it became a lot harder to ignore the elephant in the room. It was as though as soon as I got in the car there was indeed a big fat elephant sitting next to me. I named the elephant Ellis.

As hopeful as I was for a smooth ride home, it was peak hour on a Friday and Sydney traffic was bumper-to-bumper. Ellis was blocking half the windshield and breathing deliberately right down my neck, which made it incredibly difficult for me to focus on anything else. I told Ellis to please look out the window at the scenery, allow me to enjoy what was left of the *Home and Away* buzz, and assured him that we would get to know each other properly once we got home.

I swung open the front door of my shared house in Freshwater and overheard the commotion of my wage-slaved roommates cracking Coronas, gearing up for typical Friday night escapades.

Luke texted to say he'd been held up at work, so it was just Tarah and Brett in the living room, both of whom had yet to be informed of the morning's proceedings. I needed a minute alone with Ellis before facing my friends, so I pretended to be on the phone, waved a quick 'hello,' and ran upstairs. Bailing out of social events for consecutive weekends in a row is frowned upon in Australia, deeply frowned upon. I'd been copping shade because of it for weeks."Not feeling great" without elaboration or some kind of proof understandably started to come off as quite offensive. I'd tried to explain that the last time we went out, my hangover lasted a solid week, left me spiritless and functioning with the energy of a 93- year-old woman, but they weren't having any of that either.

I paused in the stairwell and spied on my friends. They seemed happy. They were playing house music, the doors were open and a breeze flowed through the living room. The liberal crunch of cheesy Doritos filled the air as potential drinking venues were discussed. While wondering if I was even allowed to eat Doritos anymore, Ellis became gradually more petulant and told me it was time to face the music. "Hold back the tears, boss, just rip off the band-aid," he said while shoving me down the stairs. "Ah-hem, Guys?" I stammered, "Hey... you know how I haven't been feeling great lately?" I paused for a few seconds, attempted desperately to push the giant lump back down my throat, wiped away a single tear, and pretended I had some dust in my eye. The looks on my friends' faces were the looks I dreaded, the faces that solidified my new found reality. They were quiet, not because they were being polite (Australians love talking over one another), but because they could see I was scared. They could tell something was wrong. So after a few minutes of everyone silently standing around, waiting for me to say something, I just spat it out. "Turns out I've got full-blown type 1 diabetes."

From there, I burst into tears, dived head first onto Mum's hand-me-down teal leather sofa, buried my head in cushions, and let it all out. Tarah swooped in beside me and started petting my head. Brett crouched down on the floor and held my hand. They both just kept saying it was going to be OK and that they were there for me. Tarah asked if I was hungry, which I was. I hadn't eaten all day and told them that was the result of there now being a whole fucking process that needed to happen before I could have any food at all. They asked lots of questions, most of which I didn't know how to answer. "All I know is that apparently, I have to inject myself with insulin before eating from now on, since my body isn't producing it on its own anymore."

Tarah's been my best friend since I was 13. She's as caring as she is fearless and has helped me navigate most of the trickier times in my life. She held up the needle and inspected it with more intrigue than concern.

"Do you know how to give yourself an injection, babe?" she asked.

I vaguely remembered that it was pretty straightforward, but that didn't make me any more confident. At the end of the day, it was still a fucking needle. Tarah dusted me off with some words of encouragement, "We've got you, Alex, it can't be that hard. Show us what you remember and we'll figure this shit out together."

I emptied the bag of contraptions onto the coffee table, everyone leaned in and rolled up their sleeves.

"The first bit is the glucose monitor…"

I turned it on and it started humming like an alien. I wondered what that meant. We fiddled around with the devices like a bunch of chimps attempting to get a snack out of an anthill. It all started to feel a little less daunting with the homies by my side. My mate Brett is a carpenter by trade, rugged and resilient to the eye, but an absolute bunny rabbit at heart. He can fix or build just about anything and is always up for a challenge. Brett started to get a bit fiddly with the monitor, flipped it over, pressed some buttons and got it making another weird noise.

"Just wait man, give it a second, it's probably warming up…" he said.

Suddenly, the words "apply drop" appeared on the screen. Oh, boom. That's what we're after.

"Hold up, my hands have gotta be clean before I can start," I said, whizzing over to the kitchen sink quickly before returning to the couch to get pricked-up. "Mother Fucking OUCH."

I placed that pea-sized drop of blood onto the test strip, which resulted in more mysterious humming noises and haptic feedback. Ninnnnnggggg ninnnggggggg, went the machine, whizzing and whirring like R2-D2. "14.5 mmol/L (261 mg/dl)... is that good?" Asked Brett anxiously. "No idea," I replied, "but this morning it was 41.3 mmol/L (738 mg/dl). Can you Google what normal blood sugar is?" Brett typed away. His eyes lit up as he found the right information. "Got it! Between 4 and 6 mmol/L (72 and 108 mg/dl). OK, so it's come down a bit. That's good, right?" We all gathered around like a group of pre-teens playing a game of Hungry Hippos to study the WebMD article Brett had found. Nobody had played the game before, but we were figuring it out together. Once we had some proper context for my blood sugar levels, it was time to measure out the right amount of insulin and inject it into my body.

Christ.

Fumbling around in my bag of tricks, I extracted a hypodermic needle from the box. I pulled off the sticker and screwed it onto the end of a bright orange disposable flex pen that goes by the name Nova Rapid. I recalled

Elma, my diabetes educator, saying that I should pinch the skin while injecting. She said it's much less painful if you grab the fattiest part of your belly and push it up like a little marshmallow cushion before pushing in the needle. A nifty nugget of wisdom, I thought.

Right. We were ready to do the thing. I leaned back on the couch with my shirt pulled up and was successfully pinching and holding with one hand. Unfortunately, I may as well have been conducting a fucking orchestra with the pen-holding hand. As soon as the needle came in close range to the contact point, it just bounced right back up, like an automatic reflex. To give you an image, I likely resembled a paralyzed bird lying on her back, desperately trying to reach a small piece of bread on her stomach, but without the ability to sit up or the dexterity of functioning fingers. I once read that the most difficult form of suicide is by stabbing yourself in the stomach, which made some sense to me at that moment. Something internal rejects the notion almost entirely, causing your arm to freeze up, procrastinate and do anything but force that knife into your tummy.

Frustrated yet starving, I knew I had to prevail. With determination, vigor, and to a chorus of cheers from Brett and Tarah, I kicked the coffee table away and created a little more room to move. I took several deep breaths and forced the needle right up close to the marshmallow. I got the insulin pen so close, it was practically hovering over the pinched belly fat; stationed right above it, circling the marshmallow like a helicopter ready to land.

But I just couldn't land the bitch.

A sudden wave of depression washed over me. I was struggling to wrap my head around the fact that I would have to do this every time I ate any food for the rest of my life. It was all so etch and scary and unfamiliar. Tarah caught on to my rising frustration and took control over the situation. "Put that shit down man and give me a hug," she said.

"Now, cry it out baby because you have every right to. We'll get through this together." She then told me I was an idiot (which in Australia is an enormous compliment as long as it comes from someone you love) and that there was nothing I couldn't handle. Via the help of my friends, the needle finally went in for a successful first injection. We did it together. It was pretty fucking cute in the end, and it didn't even hurt. In fact, it felt good to rip off the band-aid and I knew the next one would be easier. I finally ate something and as a show of gratitude for their noble efforts, performed an A cappella version of the song, "With a Little Help From My Friends," to Tarah and Brett, which was something they'd never have tolerated had I not been recently diagnosed with a chronic disease.

4

THERE'S A CHANCE.
THERE'S A POINT.
THERE'S A REASON.

In the days that followed the big day of diabetic discovery, I mostly kept to myself and focused on wrapping my head around it all. Let's say it was a period of processing. Something pretty nuts happened during this processing period though, as if things weren't nutty enough already. A director from *Home and Away* called with an offer to come back as a series regular! I repeat - a series regular! We're talking about poster status here, guys! A lead acting role on *Home and Away* for a miniMum of three years! Good LORD. Can you even believe it?!

An actor can go months or years without even a nibble of interest or traction, but like they say,. "good things happen when you least expect it." I'd been hustling for an offer like this for 10 years and I'll admit with full certainty that I was not expecting that call in the slightest.

Naturally, this offer was tremendously alluring for a number of reasons. However, there was something holding me back: I already had a plan in place. Months earlier, on the last day of pilot season in Los Angeles, I drove to Beverly Hills and paid my agents a visit. We didn't spend a lot of time discussing the 40 odd auditions that amounted to absolutely nothing, but rather the epiphany I'd had the night previous. I realized that in spite of my luck (or lack thereof), there wasn't a single place I'd been that made me feel more alive than the nut-house that was Hollywood. The rejection, albeit a-plenty, lit a fire in my soul. I knew with full certainty that LA was where I wanted and needed to be, where it felt like anything could happen. So that day, I established the plan to return to LA and months later, that plan remained the same... But what's that saying about, "a bird in the hand?" Even if it meant I'd postpone my pilgrimage to California, was it not crazy to pass up on a consistent, paying gig, something I'd been working toward for years now? It was time to phone a friend, and in times like these, there was only one friend I considered calling: Mum.

Pippy G was understandably over the moon. It was she who knew more than anyone just how badly I'd always dreamt of a full-time acting job. Pippy's always been my biggest support. She sat front and centre at every school musical, found my first agent, drove me to auditions before I had a license, provided her shoulder after every knock back and has forever reminded me that my day would come. She understood my reticence to put off chasing my dreams on the other side of the world, but the mother in her couldn't deny that taking a job on *Home and Away* after just being diagnosed with a chronic and complicated disease sounded like a fairly prudent move. She reminded me that consistent acting work was incredibly hard to come by, that not only would the job give me a break from the 10 year hustle, it would give me time to adapt to life with diabetes. Mum had some solid points. I had been on the hunt for regular acting work for a very long time. I'd been playing the game long enough to know that if, by some miracle, a job did come up, you'd be wise to take it.

I hung up the phone, feeling slightly dejected after Pippy G's enthusiasm for safety and reliability. I considered the numerous conversations we'd had about "risking it for the biscuit" in LA, but now she seemed too reluctant to allow the plan into the equation anymore. It was as though it had been replaced by diabetes, which didn't sit well with me. I understood her points, but knew wholeheartedly I'd have to make the decision myself.

Flustered and very revved up, I wandered barefoot outside. It was a damn-near-perfect day in Freshwater. The roommates were all at work, which gave me some much-needed peace and quiet to let it all marinate. I prepared myself for what would be the moment of clarity. I cleared a pile of leaves and spider webs off the crappy old patio furniture and stared at a couple of Lorikeets who had perched down beside me for moral support, right on cue. I lit myself a private decision-making-ciggie, (a filthy habit, but one that I refused to kick) ignored the judgement from the colorful birds, threw my head back and looked to the sky... for a sign? Like they do in the movies? Ahhhh. Blinded. Too bright. I aborted the sky search and closed my eyes in hopes the answer would come from within. I was irrationally perturbed with Mum for reminding me of my new disease and her suggestion that it may have some sort of influence over my life. Before all this happened, the plan was always to get over to LA as quickly as possible to embark upon the challenge to the highest degree... to feel scared. I believed in myself before diabetes and I still believed in myself. If my recent diagnosis kept me from my path, what else would it keep me from doing? What kind of life would that create? How much regret could I be prepared to live with?

How is this even a question?

I decided that diabetes didn't have a say in my dreams. I would be forever grateful to *Home and Away* for the experiences and education it offered me in the past and for the future opportunity it presented, but my heart was set. I wanted to fly as high as I possibly could and without delay. I decided to focus on some different advice Mum gave me in the past: "Go for it." She's the one who always encouraged me to follow my dreams. When I called her to explain my decision, she was understandably a little spooked by the uncertainty of it all, but wasn't surprised in the slightest and offered her unconditional support, as she always has.

After respectfully declining the generous offer, I had a little under three months left to hustle as much money as I could before heading back to LA. I'd always been envious of the actors who've never had to pull a beer or sell jeans to make ends meet. I'd wondered what that must have been like, but that wasn't my story. I'm a big believer in setting goals, that's another thing Mum taught me. It doesn't matter what you're going through, be it change or anxiety, being unemployed or broke, or an existential crisis, goals give us something to work towards. They give us focus on what's ahead as opposed to what may or may not be sitting right in front of us. You chip away, and slowly you'll start to see you're moving closer towards that goal. The progression, as slow as it may be, offers encouragement and a sense of purpose. Once you see this in action, you're more inclined to continue on. Doesn't matter how you get there, just as long as you're on your way.

I'd had a few jobs since leaving school five years prior, the first of which were in pubs. It was fun for a while. It felt like I was living that gritty artistic lifestyle. But after spending a good couple years placing patties onto buns, breaking glasses, dodging local slime-balls and getting home after midnight covered head to toe in beer, I decided my career as a bartender had come to an end. My next day-job was in retail. Retail was great for me because I wouldn't have to pay for clothes, which I couldn't afford, and it helped me to maintain my desired chic and edgy appearance. Sass & Bide at that point was the cat's pajamas as far as young Sydney women's fashion was concerned. The store had a VIP change room to entice traveling celebrities to pop in for a purchase and being in Paddington (a ritzy Sydney suburb), they often did. It was always quite exciting when someone famous came in, mostly because if I caught them first (or the manager was out on her lunch break), I would make a tremendous amount of commission.

I got pretty good at figuring out, within five minutes or so, who was going to be spending five grand and who was just in to grab a t-shirt. Our sales commissions were given to us as "Sass Dollars" and could only be spent on clothes in the store, which was a clever way for the company to give sales commissions without actually spending any money. Over the years I had collected quite an elaborate pile of garments. I kept them clean and once a dress was out of season I would sell it on Ebay. It was a sneaky little system I actually used to pay for my first trip to Hollywood. Myself and some fellow employees created aliases on Ebay because the bosses were onto us. On our lunch breaks we would quickly package up our secondhand items and ship them off to the highest bidder. The way I saw it, we were recycling the glorious garments that had already served their purpose and would continue to bring stylish happiness to others. Recycling is a good thing! Also, what the hell else was I going to do with 38 studded boob tubes?

By the time I was diagnosed, I had left Sass & Bide and moved on just a few doors down to a store called Bassike, this time selling $400 jeans and organic cotton t-shirts for $120 a pop. I would have stayed at Sass, but they weren't giving me enough shifts and my "extra-curricular" income wasn't making ends meet anymore. Bassike needed someone who could zip around their three Sydney stores as a sort of helicopter sales assistant. I drove the length of Sydney on a daily basis, giving assistance to whichever store needed it the most. It was pretty exhausting, and the store was quieter than Sass & Bide. There weren't as many customers and sometimes I was just there by myself, which was a tad lonely at times.

One of the Bassike stores was in Avalon a trendy, yet intimidating suburb on the Northern Beaches. Shortly after I was diagnosed, Mum came down to meet me for lunch. We were looking at menus in an outstandingly overpriced hipster cafe just a few doors down from Bassike. It's difficult to avoid places like these in Sydney. This particular one was called the "Nourished Whole-Food Cafe." I had (and have) a love-hate relationship with eateries like this. I love them because typically they serve fresh, healthy food that I trust will be supporting my inner and outer temple. I hate them because, for some reason, these kinds of establishments insist on naming themselves in the form of some kind of nauseating inspirational life quote. They even went so far as to name each dish in a similar way, such as the "I Am Grateful" bowl or the "Enlighten Me" sandwich. Call me pessimistic, but sometimes I just want to enjoy a $27 sandwich without being told how I should be feeling while I eat it.

My go-to coffee order was a soy latte with a scoop of honey. I'd made very few changes to my diet during those early stages, but the day prior I'd had a blood sugar spike after my usual caffeinated treat. Assuming honey was to blame, I looked around for some stevia (a sugar alternative). I politely asked one of the staff where I might find what I was looking for, "Hi there, sorry to bother you, I was just wondering where you keep the sugar-free sweeteners..."

"We only carry nature's raw and organic brown sugar," he replied in a jarringly patronizing tone. I could have been ultra sensitive at the time, but his response made me feel as though I'd just asked him for cocaine or a weapon. After establishing that he couldn't help me, he turned away abruptly and got back to adding chlorophyll to a communal jug of alkaline "spirit" water. I knew we should have just gone to the kebab shop.

Any other day I wouldn't have let this guy's tone get under my skin, but it was my first week since being diagnosed and he made me feel embarrassed and singled out. I told him I'd just been diagnosed with diabetes and gave him my two cents, which he didn't seem to care about in the slightest. Fair enough, asshole.

As I took the first bite of my meal, I sadly remembered that I would need to inject. I wasn't yet confident enough to shoot up in public, so I scanned the cafe for a restroom. There wasn't one, of course, so I grabbed my insulin pen and walked back to Bassike to use the staff bathroom. Once there, I realized I had forgotten a needle. Glassy-eyed, I walked back to the cafe to grab my purse. Mum seemed to think I should just do it there, likely because she didn't want me to feel ashamed or perhaps to get an idea of how I was managing with the whole injection thing, you know, before moving to America.

I weighed up the pros and cons.

The pros were:

1. Obviously, I would be able to eat my meal while it was still hot and continue a conversation with Mum.

2. I'd just whip it out and stab it in like a ninja, so professionally that nobody would even blink.

3. Or if they did, they would maybe be impressed and curious. "Look at that cool girl over there, she just injected something so quickly. She wasn't even looking, what a legend, dealing with whatever she has with such ease and style."

The cons were thus, and had to be considered:

1. Risk of dropping needles all over the floor in front of everyone.

2. Risk of looking like some sort of dangerous drug addict, scaring onlooking school kids and grandparents.

3. Having a bad injection episode and scaring Pippy G into thinking I wasn't ready to relocate to the other side of the world.

I decided to go ahead and administer my first public injection and that the needle would go in my stomach. I had created quite an audience, as I needed about three or four attempts to get it right. I hoped I would eventually get more confident with the whole process, but that day I had the confidence of a wingless, uncoordinated sparrow. The whole performance left me feeling the opposite of hungry, but I remembered that once the drugs were under the skin, the food had to follow. So, like a toddler who had been told they must finish their dinner, I kept my head low to the plate and did my best to finish the meal.

Without saying anything, Mum took my hand and showed me her phone. She'd just purchased a bunch of mini stevia dispensers on Amazon. "You can keep one in your handbag," she said. "I'm so proud of you, Al, you're already getting the hang of it and before you know it you'll be a pro." I knew she was right. Mum's words helped a hell of a lot. They made me feel like she was OK with me leaving and that for every inconvenience this disease caused, there would be something or someone that came along to make things a little better. It might take time, but I'd eventually make this thing my bitch. Laughing and crying (both of us) Mum indicated that we should leave, and like Bert and Ernie, we bounced.

5

MY FIRST HYPO/BECOMING A CYBORG

Right. So I made it through week two. It was Friday night and the roommates had politely respected my decision to stay in. Candles were lit, roast chicken and veggies went down like a treat and I felt clean and sleek after a shower and a face mask for my nuclear acne. The plan was to watch as many episodes of *Friends* as possible before slipping off to the land of sleep, where bodies heal and beauty blossoms. While my mates were out having drinks and getting wrinkles, I was at home, high and mighty, aging backwards like Benjamin Button. A selfie came through from Tarah, who looked about four beers-deep. I sent one back, "Wish I was there!" Except I didn't, not really. Bit too soon. Baby steps.

I was enjoying the episode where Chandler and Joey got a baby chicken and duck as pets when, suddenly, a wave of unexpected hunger washed over me. This seemed peculiar considering I'd eaten a rather large meal about an hour earlier. In any case, I wasn't about to bother with any more food as I was too tired to deal with the insulin procedure and I didn't want to fuck with my blood sugar right before bed. Mind over matter, I chugged a glass of water instead.

Everything seemed fine for a while, until I started to notice that my laptop screen suddenly appeared about 10 lumens brighter than it was just minutes ago. My eyes were having trouble focusing on the screen. While attempting to adjust the brightness, I started to feel a bit shaky, slightly disoriented, unsettled. I went for a toilet run, had a quick, nervous pee in the dark and thought perhaps a splash of water to the face would do the trick. It didn't. I started feeling very dizzy and thought to myself, "Christ, no one else is home," as I carefully slid down to the bathroom floor in hopes of avoiding a fall.

I had recently christened my glucose monitor, "Glen"... I thought Glen was quite a comforting name, like a handyman-type-guy who will never hesitate to fix something for you, or give you a lift to the airport. Glen was the only thing that could clarify whether or not I'd now found myself in a diabetic related predicament or if, in fact, this was just some kind of passing spell. I crawled to the bedside table from the bathroom floor and attempted my first ever half-naked, horizontal finger prick. The reading was 2.3 mmol/L (41.4 mg/dl). Christ. "That can't be good," I thought. Glen had yet to give me a number below 4 mmol/L (72 mg/dl). It became fairly and quickly apparent that I had to be experiencing symptoms of low blood sugar. 2.3 mmol/L (41.4 mg/dl) was very low, and if it went any lower, there was a chance I could fall into a diabetic coma which, if left untreated, could result in brain damage or even kill me. If my blood sugar kept dropping (and I had no idea whether or not they would) and I passed out, I'd be pretty screwed. I was home alone, without anyone to find me and jab me with the glucagon pen which is required in severe cases of hypoglycemia (aka hypo).

The panic set in. I started to perspire at a frightening pace, threw on the nearest T-shirt and tried not to think about what scary things might have been happening in my body. This was my first time experiencing a very real hypo and it was by far the most terrifyingly bizarre combination of sensations I'd ever felt. My body got lighter by the second, my legs were wobbly. I somehow felt like I was on speed and like I could faint at any second. The panic washed over me with such intensity that I couldn't bring myself to think straight for even a moment. The only thought my mind could fixate on was food. I was suddenly hungrier than I'd ever been in my entire life, starving, instantly malnourished, but my brain wasn't helping me find a solution. Instead, it malfunctioned, glitched, struggled so hard to stay powered up that it couldn't tell me the nearest sugar I needed was right next to my bed, or downstairs in the kitchen. My brain seemed to have reverted to some lizard-state, or dream like haze, one that instead reminded me of a bag of trail mix I'd left in the car, parked all the way out on the street.

I flew down the stairs, right past the fully stocked kitchen and searched frantically for my car keys. My brain didn't help me find the keys either and I started to cry while manically walking around in circles. It felt like my entire system was shutting down now and frighteningly fast. The seconds felt like hours until I finally found my handbag, which was by the front door - where I always left it - and dug out my keys. On the walk out to the car I remember feeling like a ghost, like I could have blown away in the wind.

As I finally reached the car and jerked open the driver-side door, I noticed a jar of jelly beans. Mum had put them there, bless her soul and suddenly I felt like she was with me and that everything was going to be OK. I quickly grabbed the jar like a fiend, but my hands weren't working properly as I couldn't seem to manage prying off the lid. "Come on, hands. Fuck," I thought, just before successfully and violently popping the jar open and sending rainbow-colored pellets exploding everywhere except my mouth.

"Fuck it." I thought, and started eating them off the ground.

Sat in the gutter, I chewed and swallowed full mouthfuls of jellybeans as quickly as I could and then got to work on the trail mix. It felt as though I was eating food for the first time in my life or that I had been starved for weeks. I could taste every single morsel separately. It all tasted so incredibly good. Even while consuming the trail-mix like a crazed gorilla, I could still differentiate the distinct flavor of each nut, raisin and delectable chocolate chip as the glucose pulsed the pleasure sensors in my brain back to life. After shoveling down about half of the 2-pound bag, the fog began to lift. My heart rate slowed, my hands were no longer shaking, the strength came back to my legs and the clarity came back to my mind. I still felt weak, depleted, exhausted and heavy, but thankfully I felt very much alive again.

As everything gradually came back into focus, I noticed a hesitant-looking couple taking their dog for a late night stroll. My car doors were swung open, fog-lights on, and I was bawling in my undies in the gutter, demolishing cashews like a malnourished and potentially dangerous chimpanzee. "Everything OK?" asked the man, while discretely signaling for his girlfriend to stay back.

I was OK. A little shaken and now embarrassed, but OK nonetheless. I waited for them to round the corner before heading back inside.

REFRESHER:
(BECAUSE THIS SHIT'S IMPORTANT)

Hypoglycemia, or 'low blood sugar,' is a condition that occurs when your blood sugar (glucose) levels are lower than normal. In order for our bodies to function, we require a hormone called insulin which delivers vital nutrients from the food we eat to our muscles, liver and kidneys. For people without type 1 Diabetes (T1D), the pancreas automatically produces the exact amount of insulin required to account for the glucose (food) we have eaten. People with T1D depend on synthetic insulin injections as the pancreas has ceased to produce insulin on its own. Once injected, the insulin begins the irreversible process of bringing down your blood sugar, which means that if you haven't eaten enough food for the insulin to work with, your existing blood sugar levels will crash. This crash will continue until the entire body shuts down, unless it's brought back to balance with the glucose your body desperately needs.

As you can probably imagine, administering synthetic insulin is a bit of a tightrope walk. We're essentially manually simulating an automatic biological process that took our bodies millions of years to evolve, and if we get it wrong it can have life-threatening consequences. Hypoglycemia can occur with various levels of severity but when it's bad, it feels like you're becoming increasingly weightless, mentally impaired, or slipping away on a bad acid trip. Put more simply, it feels like you're dying. Back when I had my first "hypo," that's pretty much all I understood about the whole thing. Low blood sugar + too much insulin = feelings of being hit by bus, potential coma, possible death. Day definitely ruined.

Great. I was really getting the hang of it.

Doing my 'insulin math' became a daily chore. Elma, my diabetes educator had given me a reference book to help with making these calculations. I gave the book a go, but decided it wasn't that useful. The first time I ate chicken and veggies, everything was fine, but when I tried to repeat the same thing the next night it was way off. I learned that keeping balanced blood sugar was dependent on many variables outside of insulin and food alone and that the effects of insulin are fairly individualistic. I realized through my own experience, and with little help or advice from medical professionals, that I was in fact highly sensitive to insulin. I only needed very small doses at a time. Despite everything I started to learn, having that hypo left me feeling defeated and overwhelmed. My confidence was knocked back into the ether as I realized this thing was kind of complex. It was something I would have to think about all day every day for the rest of my life. I thought I knew what I was doing. I thought I understood, but there was so much more to untangle and so much ahead of me yet to learn.

Post-hypo, Mum was understandably keen to find a better way for me to manage my blood sugar, so she bought me something called a Continuous Glucose Monitor (CGM). This, in theory, sounded great. It would give me blood sugar readings every five minutes and I wouldn't have to do a thing. Unfortunately, my mind instantly went back to the alien-looking devices that Elma had shown me a couple weeks earlier. Remember, the wearable remote control things hanging off the rubber, faux-belly that scared the Bejeesus out of me? I still wasn't super keen, as you might imagine.

By the time my cyborg stomach apparatus arrived, Luke and I had moved home to Lane Cove to live with Pippy. Our lease was up in Freshwater and we were set to move over to the States in the next couple of months. At the time, CGMs in general were fairly new to the market. The instructions mentioned that the sensor could only be attached to the stomach area which, in my opinion, was the absolute worst place for a miniature computer. What if I wanted to wear a cropped t-shirt? Show off my abs? Wear a bikini for Christ's sakes? How was I going to do pilates? How could I lie on my stomach without potentially ripping the damn thing out? I was negging the device emotionally before I even put it on. I was fine with accepting the needles, the finger pricking, the blatant fact that I was now a social leper (otherwise known as a person with type 1 diabetes), but I was absolutely in no rush to start wearing something on my skin that reminded me every day of that fact.

In the end, however, I tried it out. I did it mostly for Mum. I knew how concerned she was as my departure date edged closer and closer. I knew what a fright my hypo gave her and that wearing the silly/scary device might make her feel better about my decision to relocate so far away from her watchful and caring eye.

So, of course, the initial insertion process was a whole thing. Mum had obviously watched and studied all the relevant YouTube videos and read all the instructions. I tried tremendously hard to be patient, to keep my cool even though I knew deep down I wasn't ready for it. We inserted the sensor into the skin on my stomach. I likely hit a nerve or blood vessel or something as I noticed blood started to seep out from under the adhesive. According to the instruction manual, this was reasonably normal, though I had to disagree. There didn't seem to be a single normal thing whatsoever about this experience. We then needed to hook the sensor up to a bluetooth device. The bluetooth receiver was the size of a cassette tape and, in order for it to work properly, I had to remain within 50 feet of the device, like a wifi router.

I had become a wifi router.

The next day, I went to a pump class at the gym with my insanely fit sister. For those of you unfamiliar with a pump class, it's basically aerobics with weights and techno music. A vivacious lady, in head to toe Lululemon, led the class. She stood on a makeshift podium at the front of the studio, fastened her microphone headpiece, clicked play on a playlist full of the latest house/techno music, and told us we were all beautiful and worth it.

Caley, my super-fit and hot little sister, was pumping an absurdly disproportionate amount of weight with mind-blowing ease. Caley is tiny. She's one of those people you might actually worry about stepping on simply because you didn't know she was there. You could put her in your pocket.

She's a snack, but she makes up for her physical minia-ture-ness with a spiritual drive, passion and love so robust, she radiates it into every room she enters. She is a magic elf with the strength and tenacity of an olympic athlete.

Caley, being by far the most experienced at pump classes, constantly glanced back and gave me encourag-ing looks. Great - Alex is still alive - check. Her cyborg device is still firmly attached - check. I began to slightly enjoy myself. I wasn't keeping up with the others, but no-body seemed to mind that when everybody went left, I went right. I was feeling very appreciative for the uplifting environment and some quality time with my sibling.

My robot stomach, apart from making me look like a senior citizen with no bowel control, was a literal pain in my ass (stomach). I felt the wire under my skin every time I moved my abdomen, as though I had a metal splinter wedged in there and gently tickled and scraped my internal organs. Horrendous. After the class finished, we debriefed over a latte downstairs. Caley could tell I was already frustrated with the CGM, but suggested that my new friend might take a little getting used to and maybe the benefits would eventually outweigh the inconvenience. I nodded along knowing full well that Caley tended to be right about these things. I resolved to be patient for at least a little longer.

I slept terribly that night. Every time I rolled over, the device found a way of pissing me off. It would rub on the mattress and I couldn't seem to get comfortable at all. There were many minor annoyances I could tolerate from this CGM, but losing out on sleep was something I simply could not abide. On top of this, the device readings seemed to be consistently inaccurate when I double checked using Glen. Could it be a faulty device? Was the technology really advanced enough to be relied upon yet? The fact that I even had to ask these questions made me question whether or not this experiment was worth it at all and, thus, my first try using a continuous glucose monitor promptly came to an end. I felt bad for Mum, as I assumed the device wasn't cheap, but I simply wasn't ready for it. Despite the fact that the device might have improved my life, it made me feel claustrophobic and reminded me of my "sickness" more frequently than I preferred. So, as quickly as I'd plugged it into my stomach, the continuous glucose monitor went back onto the pile and I went back on with my life.

6

WONDERLAND

As the old saying goes, "when it rains, it pours." Suddenly, it started pouring! With excellent stuff! The *Home and Away* guest role was the only gig I'd booked in well over a year, but lo and behold... I booked another one! I couldn't help but wonder if perhaps the newly altered, "edgier" me might in fact be contributing to my overall appeal!?

Hey man! I'll take it!!

It's pointless to question why things happen - you've just gotta run with it when they do. Take the bull by his pointy horns and charge forward into the unknown, full speed ahead! Or something like that...

The role was to play "Jodie the swimmer" on the new Australian show *Wonderland*, which was filmed in the eastern suburbs of Sydney. As per usual, I was incredibly excited for another opportunity to "do ma thang" and meet a new cast and crew. I was in a fairly good place going into this gig. I hadn't had too many more hypos after that scary first one and I was beginning to feel as though perhaps this diabetes thing wasn't going to be so bad after all. To be completely honest, I was actually feeling incredibly stoked with myself. I felt like a winner. I'd just been diagnosed with a fairly hefty life-altering disease, yet I was still me! You know?! Diabetes?! Not even a problem.

It was just a small role, as all of my acting jobs had been thus far, but as they say, "there are no small parts, only small actors." I had yet to land a role so significant that I felt like a proper part of the crew. I remember I used to fantasize about the day I'd book a role important enough to require me to keep a toothbrush in the make-up trailer. Sounds weird but it's something I've taken notice of over the years. A designated trailer toothbrush is an unmistakable sign that you really belong there.

That said, being a guest star for an episode or two was exhilarating. It made you a sort-of travelling artistic mercenary. You rolled in, shot your scenes - hoping to god you didn't fuck them up - then you left. The regular actors would be working non-stop, and the guest stars were in and out so quickly that it was understandably pretty much impossible to make friends or creative acquaintances, but I did my best. I spoke when I was spoken to and I stayed out of the way when I wasn't needed. I always aimed to be perceived as the mysterious guest star who just chills on the sideline, and then blows everyone away when it was my moment. I didn't want to be the overly eager, potentially annoying guest star who everybody called a diva. An undeserving diva, you never ever wanna be one of those. "Just be cool, Al," that's what I used to tell myself. Be cool, do your thing and one day you might be the star of the show. Everybody will know your name and it will be necessary and expected for you to have that trailer toothbrush.

On the first day of shooting, I arrived just a TAD earlier than my designated call time. In fact, I had actually arrived an hour earlier than my call time. To avoid appearing too keen, I decided to park nearby and enjoy a latte where no one could see me. A little closer to my actual call time, I made my way over to base camp and sat at an empty table out of the way yet easily visible. When someone came looking for "Jodie the swimmer", my character, I would be easy to locate and appear professional yet chilled as opposed to awkwardly eager, hovering around the action like a bad smell.

While waiting for instructions, desperate not to seem like a total Nancy-no-friends, I emptied my backpack onto the table and began reorganizing its contents. Unfortunately, it just so happened that I had forgotten to zip up all the needles in the front part of my backpack. This resulted in a cascade of junkie-looking diabetes supplies falling onto the floor in front of the helpful AD (assistant Director), who meanwhile silently approached to invite me to hair and makeup. Oh, and a couple of bonus tampons fell out too. Brilliant.

Jake was the unlucky AD assigned to me and he offered to help pick up my explosion of drug paraphernalia. I was mortified that Jake might accidentally grab a used needle and spike himself so I manically got down on my hands and knees and scooped everything up.

"I got it! Thanks so much. Sorry about this! Have you been working here long?!" Kill me, kill me, kill me.

Once seated in the makeup chair, doing my best to chime in to already existing conversations, I noticed and admired one of the stars of the show brushing her teeth with her very own trailer toothbrush. It was a spiritual and welcome reminder of what matters in life. My makeup session was quick, as we were shooting a beach swimming scene and the makeup needed was minimal.

Jake suggested I grab myself some breakfast while I waited to be called to set, so I sat back down at my old empty table and focused on enjoying my meal like a normal person. While taking a bite of my breakfast I remembered I had diabetes, so I carefully whipped out my equipment and got going with the pre-meal injection procedure. As I did so, one of the main actors in the series, Jane, who I admired and met previously on *Home and Away*, approached me to say hello. This I wasn't expecting, but was absolutely delighted. She noticed the insulin pen, Glen the glucose monitor, and the rest of my nicknacks. She politely and with genuine interest asked what I was doing. This was likely the first time I had explained my condition to someone I wasn't well acquainted with and it felt pretty good to have someone as cool as Jane appear genuinely interested. She had a seat with me and I told her a bit about my diagnosis as we chatted over breakfast. It feels weird to say this, but I really don't think our conversation would have gone on nearly as long without such a captivating starting point.

I couldn't help but wonder if diabetes had somehow made me more interesting? Interesting!

After shooting my ocean-side scene, everyone migrated back to base camp to sit down for lunch. Lunch time on any film or TV set is generally less of a social event and more of a frantic refuel. Usually, I wouldn't require company during a meal - on any normal day I am absolutely fulfilled by my own company and sometimes actually prefer it. Today was different. I was out of my comfort zone. I wasn't a regular player in this production - always felt a bit on the outside looking in. I was eager to make connections and relationships with anyone who happened to be around, but I was nervous to strike up a conversation with coworkers who might just be trying to enjoy their meals in peace. Needless to say, I was quite anxious about my awkward vibe.

I stood in line at the lunch que, proud to have my first scene in the can (finished filming), wearing a dressing gown and some hotel slippers, smelling of sea-salt and sunscreen. I lathered my meal in hot sauce (as was my custom at the time) and wandered over to the dining area, scanning around for an empty table. I felt like the new kid on the block in one of those American high school films. I gazed out at the sea of foldable tables and chairs and attempted to figure out the most appropriate place to sit without appearing like I was overthinking it. Tables kept filling up at a rapid pace. Keeping my cool, I spotted an empty table at the back and bee-lined for a chair. Last to arrive for lunch were the three lead female actors, including Jane. Realizing my loner table at the back was the only one with vacant seats, I wondered if perhaps they might come and join me, you know, just because there was nowhere else to sit.

Prease be my fwiend?

Now the cool thing for me to have done here would be to mind my own business, assume the girls likely wouldn't come sit with the random guest star at the back, check with Glen, inject and eat my lunch. But I'm not cool. All I could think about was how cool it was to have something to talk about this morning with Jane, so I decided to hold off on the injection for a minute. Instead, I pretended like I was writing an email, in case I needed to explain why I hadn't touched my food. Then, if the girls did end up coming over to my loner table, I'd be able to commence the intriguing procedure in front of them in hopes that it might make me a bit interesting… which it did. They sat down with me!!! Yay!!!

As it turned out, Jane was still curious about diabetes and the other two leads of the show shared her interest. They asked me all about it. I explained and we got to talking about all sorts of stuff for the entire meal. It was pretty rad and by far the closest I'd felt to being a part of the gang. So yeah, that was the second time that day I may or may not have intentionally used my diabetes as a conversation starter. A talking point. An "in" if you will.

I suppose you could interpret this as a rather pathetic ploy OR a sneaky deception. Either way, I guess the point of this rather long winded story was to share with you that, on that day, while out of my comfort zone, I learned that type 1 diabetes is something that's actually pretty interesting to people.

Instead of feeling embarrassed about our condition, we can actually use it to our advantage. We can explain diabetes not as something that we are, but something that we have and, in doing so, we can connect with others in a way that makes us feel bigger than the disease. I learned that day on set that my new life with type 1 diabetes would be something that made me stronger, something I should never be ashamed of and something I could actually be proud of.

7

FOMO

After a few weeks' hibernation I was starting to suffer from an acute case of FOMO. 'FOMO' or 'Fear of Missing Out' is an affliction common amongst shut-in hermit-types like myself.

FOMO occurs when a hermit (a person who primarily prefers to live in seclusion from society, may also be described as a loner and or a recluse according the internet) has spent a prolonged period of time dodging social events with friends and family and hasn't left the house in several weeks except to restock the fridge. Naturally, my recent diagnosis exacerbated this tendency in me and I started to fear being excluded entirely from the outside world.

Common symptoms of FOMO often include:

1. Feeling left out of conversations

2. Noticing you are back to watching *Friends* reruns because you are well and truly up to date with all the latest films and TV shows

3. Feeling guilty for repeatedly bailing on friends

4. Detecting a deteriorating rate of invitations to social

events in general because people start to expect your declines and therefore lose interest

The internet fails to mention that a hermit isn't something you become, it's something you are, something that you have always been. I'm sure there are reluctant hermits out there who fight tooth and nail to be enthusiastic about social events, and good for them, as it's not an easy task to resist one's own nature. The bottom line is, though, hermits are unique and fascinating creatures designed specifically to immensely enjoy their own company above the company of others.

There's nothing wrong with being a hermit, far from it, in fact. I think you'll find that if you ask around, most people have a hermit friend they love and adore in spite of their hermit-ness. I am that person for all of my friends and family. I am loved and accepted and therefore object to being referred to as a loner or a recluse. I find these terms fairly on the nose, fabrications if you will, and patently untrue. I prefer to be described as either a lone wolf, a rogue leopard, or perhaps an independent yet lovable rascal. Any of these will be absolutely fine.

Anyway, there comes a time in most (not-entirely-committed) hermits' lives, where one needs to break the hermit cycle or reduce the cabin fever via an obligatory yet essential "join the world for a minute" *reset*. By doing so, a hermit can quickly rejuvenate and restore their lone-wolf status, stop the anxiety-inducing questions, and clear the deck for another good solid month or so of accepted, judgement-free solitary confinement.

The Freshwater gang was all off to a BYO (bring yer'own) warehouse party that night. I had a slight buzz going after I finished my guest spot on *Wonderland* and thought to myself *what the hell*. I knew once I got there and had a few drinks I'd be dancing on the tables and telling everyone I loved them. I missed my pals. I was 23 for God's sake, my diabetes was mostly under control and my departure date for LA was edging closer and closer. So I put my big girl pants on and braced myself for a night of alcohol-related adventures.

Something that I had yet to try since being diagnosed was drinking alcohol, or more to the point: drinking medium to large amounts of alcohol. I'll be frank: Australians like to tie one on and, when I'm feeling my least hermit-like, I too like to imbibe risky amounts of alcoholic liquid for a laugh. But I had to assume my pancreas might have something to say about it.

I recall Elma telling me that I could absolutely drink alcohol - that diabetes shouldn't change my social life, nor my ability to consume a drink or two every now and again. While I sat in that doctor's office on the day of the diagnosis, my mind was full of questions, like:

1. Would I have to stop smoking straight away?
2. Would I still be able to go out and party with my friends till all hours of the morning?

I wanted to know these things but didn't ask them when I had the chance, because...

1. I was worried I would be judged
2. I assumed that doctors and medical practitioners were rarely going to account for this kind of frowned upon behavior, and...
3. Because I was scared of what the answer might be.

Elma had instructed me to essentially drink carefully, and remember to regularly check my sugar levels while I was out. I decided to give it a go. First time for everything, right?

After trying on an absurd amount of different outfit combinations, I predictably went with the first option and felt flustered and clammy, yet relieved and rather sexy all at once. After waiting for my sweat glands to relax from the intense outfit choosing conundrum, I thought I'd earned a cool drink.

The next step would be a makeup application. I always do this while sitting cross-legged on the floor in front of the mirror. If anyone hasn't tried it, I implore you to give it a go. It gives great stability, plus ample room to rest your drink while you attack those lashes.

With a trusty vodka-soda-fresh-lime in hand, I cleared a space in the pile of rejected clothing items, hair styling products and other unidentified crap that had become my bedroom floor. I'd picked up a tip or two from the hair and makeup professionals over at *Home and Away* and *Wonderland* for covering my recent diabetic induced cystic acne. To be honest, I did a fucking good job, like a god damm porcelain doll. Nobody would ever know what lie beneath the layers of creamy concealer.

Before heading out the door, I made a point of double-checking my diabetes kit. I had assembled over the past month or so and it contained all the equipment I needed to not pass out in a coma on the dancefloor. My own little first-aid pack, if you will. I assembled it upon realization that I needed something a bit more organized to carry around, since I had pricked my fingers on used needles while fossicking for change 10 separate times in the past week. I had also embarrassingly spilled cascades of needles all over set a number of times. I was getting sick of explaining that I was actually an actor and not a wayward heroin addict.

God I've really talked this thing up… it's just a satchel really. It's small enough to fit in your purse or backpack. A very simple discovery, you might think, but boy did it make a difference to have all my bits in the same place. One thing I will mention, though, is that the kit doesn't automatically restock items once they have been used.

Feeling poised, prepared and pretty cute, I waited outside for Tarah to pick me up. My blood sugar was normal. I'd had a bite to eat before I left, as it was fairly uncommon for warehouse booze-ups to cater food and vodka cocktails didn't fill me up like they used to. Tarah said she wouldn't be leaving my side tonight. That made me feel safe. Diabetes or not, she'd always been good at that.

Damn, it felt good to be out again.

It was a perfect spring afternoon in Sydney with a gorgeous blue sky gradually turning pink and flawless wind consistency, like a fan set to low, always pointing in your direction. The air smelled of ocean, beer and an elaborate concoction of fruity colognes. The warehouse was a large split-level garage that opened onto an empty car park where guests were invited to meander in and out for ciggies and what-not. It was a very Australian indoors/outdoors sort of event. A perfect venue for my introduction back into civil society.

My alcohol intake had dropped precipitously in the last month or so and my alcohol tolerance had diminished similarly. Though I suspected this might be the case, I was going for it anyway. This was always my problem and the problem of many hermits. Once unbuckled, the sky's the limit. Luke was the DJ (another one of his many talents) and he played all my favorite tracks, which I appreciated. It was at this point that I started to feel a tad wobbly, yet exhilarated. This was possibly due to the combination of being surrounded by my gorgeous friends, the soul-igniting house music or the cool breeze flowing through this trendy, spacious garage. I think feeling liberated to be out and partying again - as though I hadn't just been diagnosed with diabetes at all - was mostly what led me back to the drinks table one or two more times than I really needed to go.

Once I had graduated from the delinquent 18-year-old who would drink anything brightly colored that came in a pack of four, my drink of choice was always vodka soda with fresh lime and lots of ice. It's clean, free from sugar and, let's be honest, it's a chic drank. Slamming a few, I noticed I had run out of soda water. After poking about in fathomless bathtubs and coolers filled with melted ice and forgotten light beers, I realized that it was that time of night where the mixers were running out. All that was available was Coke and lemonade (read: sugary death/my kryptonite).

Now, as I mentioned earlier, I was still very much in the "figuring it out" stage of this complex illness. You might assume my next move was to simply stop drinking and go home, rather than embark upon a potentially dangerous coin toss with my pancreas. My advice to anyone who might find themselves in a similar situation is to do just that, but I was 23. I was having a lovely time and my ability to think rationally had been notably distorted for obvious reasons.

Tarah and I chatted through my options over a ciggie out the back, like a couple of doctors. We reasoned that if I just had a teensy bit of sugary death (lemonade probably) with my vodka and gave myself insulin right before, I would probably be fine.

Decision made! Who needs a medical degree anyway?

Soon after, I was up on a table dancing with a vodka lemonade in hand. The night was wrapping up and, admittedly, I had overdone it. The beer goggles were on and I ran about telling everyone I loved them dearly. Tarah pulled me aside to check my sugar, as it had been an hour or so since we last did. Before moving from soda to lemonade I got a reading of 5.3 mmol/L (95 mg/dl), which is quite respectable, so I was really hoping it had stayed pretty close to that. You can guess what happened instead. Drumroll please:

I attempted to focus on the numbers on the screen.

"What does that say to you?" I asked Tarah. She replied:

"It says 27 mmol/L (486 mg/dl) I think, man, is that bad?"

"Did you say 7 mmol/L (126 mg/dl)?" I asked hopefully.

"No babe... It's 27 mmol/L (486 mg/dl)" Tarah said.

Shit. no. That's not good!

Maybe there was sugar on my finger. Sometimes this could throw the reading off. It was worth checking again. I poured a whole bottle of water over my hand this time and wiped it thoroughly. The reading was exactly the same. 27 mmol/L (486 mg/dl)

Epic fail. Time to go home.

It's amazing how quickly a bad reading could ruin my day or night. It's as though the fog cleared and I was sober in an instant. I discovered that one of the most frustrating things about living with diabetes is that one minute you can feel invincible, strong and proud of yourself for having everything under control and, the next, shattered, confused, and lost. Suddenly, you're not one of the gang, free to make choices and mistakes as you please. One shitty, unexpectedly bad reading, regardless of how happy you felt the moment before, has the ability to make you feel instantly defeated and, above all, entirely alone.

As frustrating as this experience was, I had to expect that this sort of thing might happen. I learned a lot very fast in order to avoid another experience like this.

Did you know - a diabetic body simply doesn't know how to deal with sugary drinks, even when you take insulin. Liquid enters the bloodstream much faster than food. Insulin can't keep up with coke, lemonade, fruit juice, beer, champagne or white wine. And once the sugar has burnt off (soft-drink sugar burns off lightning-quick), the insulin you took won't have any sustainable glucose left to work with, and you run the risk of crashing low, which can be even more scary. It's a dangerous mess. Interestingly, red wine and rose can actually help stabilize blood sugar. Go figure. Oh, and drinking spirits on the rocks, or with sugar-free mixers - will support someone with type 1 as kindly as rose and red wine. How intriguing - they're my favourites

It's like I'd been training for this my whole life.

I love whiskey, by the way - if anyone wants to send me some.

8

A SHRIMP IS STILL A SHRIMP

It had been about three months since I was diagnosed and I was headed to Hollywood, baby, until further notice. I packed one large suitcase to the brim, there was five grand in my bank account and I got me a tourist ESTA visa, which allowed me three months in the country to get my shit together before being kicked out. I also had a cooler bag filled with a year's supply of insulin, since I only had travel insurance which definitely wasn't going to cover anything diabetes-related in America: the land of the million-dollar doctor visit.

Luke decided to come with me and that was probably the only thing that kept Pippy G from hiding in my suitcase or following me on the next flight. Oh, and Ellis (the elephant) came along too. He'd be travelling with me for a while, so I packed some extra peanuts.

I felt sad and a bit guilty leaving my family at the airport, knowing full well how worried they must have been. But they knew I had to go. They knew I was always going to go and it would take a hell of a lot more than getting diagnosed with T1D to stop me from following my dreams.

We arrived at LAX airport bleary eyed and sleep deprived. We dusted our pants free of peanut debris and headed to our AirBnb for the next two weeks in Marina Del Rey, down near Venice Beach in California. We explored this fabulous little enclave and remarked at how friendly and interesting the area was. I could have stayed at a backpacker inn and been just as thrilled. It felt like the beginning of the rest of my life. I thought a lot less about the fact that I had very little money and a temporary visa and much more about the feeling I got that anything could happen here. I was so excited and so grateful to finally arrive in this insane city filled to the brim with fellow dreamers.

We rented the cheapest car we could find, a rather skeptical rattling piece of shit, but the guy at Sugar Palm Rentals assured us "she" was reliable and let's face it: we were in no position to argue. I took her out for a spin en route to meet my American representative team for lunch, which included, Jeff, my manager at the time and my agent, Aron.

We met at an Italian restaurant in West Hollywood. I arrived a tad early and rushed to the restroom to adjust the makeup that had dripped off my face on the walk over from the car. Unfortunately, the mirror was deliberately blurry and the lights were dim, making it impossible for a last minute spruce. I was left with no other choice but to trust in my inner beauty, charisma, and hope that our table would be situated out of direct sunlight. I waited like a puppy anticipating the arrival of her owner after a long day, fanning myself with a menu while admiring the Californian roadside chaos. I'd dreamt of this exact lunch date for a good couple of years now.

I remember the precise moment my old Australian agent called to tell me that a big U.S. agent was interested in signing me. Aron had seen a self tape I sent over from Sydney and said he saw something special in me. Naturally, I signed with them straight away. It was a big day, as you might imagine. Prior to this lunch, we'd only met in person once or twice before, but I meant it when I told them I'd be back in Los Angeles and that time had finally come.

After joining me at the table *they* said I looked *radiant*! I said they looked radiant! They asked me how I had been managing since my diagnosis. I said it had been easy as pie, and that I'd been managing well, as I didn't want them to think differently of me (fake it 'til you make it). Regardless of their sympathetic faces while watching me fiddle about with my insulin pen, I was confident that they did, in fact, consider me mostly unchanged.

Aron mentioned a few projects for which they were working on getting me auditions. I felt like live butterflies could erupt from my chest at any moment. I'd sent audition tapes for various roles remotely to the US prior to my departure and had actually gotten a bit of traction on a few. We talked about those and a number of other exciting projects that were marinating at that point.

Aron mentioned a new TV show that was casting called *The Royals*, which rang a bell. I'd heard about it because I had actually taped an audition for one of the lead characters a few weeks ago, while still in Australia. Apparently the role was still up for grabs. They'd been searching high and wide for the perfect "*Princess Eleanor*" the only daughter of a fictional English royal family.

Typically, as an actor, if you're lucky enough to have representation, you will be sent audition opportunities. You either go in and read scenes with a casting director or tape yourself and send it remotely. It's pretty rare to get the attention of the right people from a tape though, sadly. You need to really be in the room to make an impression. It's far too competitive an industry for opportunities to find you. At this point I was like a common infant shrimp bobbing along in the ocean. An ocean filled with fluorescent siamese fighting fish, brawny dependable dolphins and exquisitely elaborate octopuses as contenders. There have been more than a few moments over the years where I really examined my choice to be an actor. Why for God's sake would anyone *want* to live a life as treacherous, unreliable and soul destroying as this? You really need to be a bit insane to go after it. Luckily, I am board-certified nuts as you might have already gathered from the previous 10 chapters of this book. Kick me in the face, tell me I'll never make it, reject me over and over again. This is my great love; we're married now. 'Til death do us part.

Anyway, a shrimp is still a shrimp at the end of the day and you gotta be in it to win it. They told me Elizabeth Hurley had been cast as the Queen. Aron seemed to think I could pass for her daughter which was an unexpected ego boost as you might imagine. Despite the fact that my previous audition tape amounted to nothing, Aron was convinced they could get me another shot now that I was in Los Angeles. It seemed that my *first ever* agent/client Hollywood lunch-date was a roaring success, better than I could have imagined. I hugged them both tightly, for a little longer than was likely appropriate and was told they'd be in touch as soon as they had something for me! The drive home that afternoon was a *really* good one. It went a little something like this:

"I'm on the top of the world looking down on creation and the only explanation that I've founnndddd."

A couple of days later I went in to audition for a role on a show called *Unreal* to play the disheveled line producer of a very hip reality show. Here, I met Barbara, one of the top casting directors in LA and one of the nicest people I have ever met. After sitting in the waiting room like Blow-Joe-who-nobody-knows, surrounded by gorgeous Siamese fighting fish, Barbara called me into the audition room. She promptly managed to make me feel like she was, in fact, very interested in me (for reasons unbeknownst to me). After the audition I felt hopeful. Jeff, my manager at the time, called soon after to say that I wasn't quite right for the role. However, Barbara and the same casting team were working on another project. This happened to be *The Royals*, and she had a feeling I might be better placed there.

It's funny the way things evolve, isn't it? I'd already worked my ass off on the audition material for the role of Princess Eleanor back in Sydney when I made that first audition tape, so the scenes were still fresh(ish) in my mind. That allowed me to really double down on making the scenes as stellar as they could possibly be before going in for my second shot. When it came time to read with Barbara we spent over an hour in the room together, which was incredible as auditions usually last about 5-10 minutes. This extended session was a first for me, a highly welcomed, intoxicating first. We worked the scenes over and over, ensuring the final product was perfect. Barbara was pushing me in a way that made me feel the opposite of inadequate or pushed, but rather empowered, challenged and capable. It was an utterly electrifying experience. After what felt like the greatest free acting class and day of my life, I drove home in a sweaty purple t-shirt feeling jazzed, grateful and optimistic.

I waited a few days to find out the good news: I was definitely in the running for the role! Barbara sent my tape off to the producers of the show. They'd take it from there. This next stage was fairly excruciating, to put it lightly. The old waiting game again, which I was familiar with of course. The stakes, however, had never been this high. Never had I wanted anything more in my *entire life*. This would be my dream job, everything I had imagined and so much more.

Seconds passed like hours, days like weeks. Luke and I focused on finding a place to live and I was grateful for the task with which to distract myself. With no credit rating, no visa, or local rental references, it was slim pickings, but this was LA after all. The land of dodging, weaving, and squirming. There's always somebody out there who's willing to bend the rules for a price of course. You've just gotta find them. We started calling around and took care to mention that we would pay cash, sir - please? After a couple of days of nobody getting back to us, we had a nibble from a bossy lady named Barb. She told us to meet her tomorrow at 1 p.m. sharp and bring the first three months rent, in cash.

We could be on here, guys.

We desperately didn't want to fuck this one up - this might be our only shot at a more permanent living situation. We arrived 30 minutes early, found an ATM and took out the large amount of cash required. We weren't able to withdraw it all in one go, however, so we did it in three or four separate transactions, costing about $8 each, which is highway robbery, by the way. In Australia, it's the equivalent of about $1.50 US. We grabbed something disgusting yet refreshing from a nearby Starbucks, parked the car in the shade and waited with bated breath for the mysterious Barb. At around 1:45 p.m. we were almost run over by a very swanky apple-red Mercedes blaring Katy Perry at an intense volume. Out popped Barb, dressed head to toe in pink and purple and flustered as hell. She slammed her vehicle into park across the entire drive way of the building. She blocked three or four vacant spots presumably designated for residents and then hurried us inside as though there was a very important appointment across town and she was late for it.

Barb was sweating, profusely to the point that I wished I had a cool drink to offer her. Barb had a lot to say and very little time to say it so we smiled, nodded and agreed with everything she said. Then we signed a crumbled, lipstick-smeared piece of paper, handed over the wad of cash and assured her the next payment would be waiting in the form of a check.

Interestingly, for readers outside the States, in America they use checks for everything. It's the only place I've been to that loves checks this much. It's literally a check for everything over here. Very odd and old-fashioned. I actually saw someone pay for groceries with a check. I'm not even shitting you.

But nevertheless, we now had somewhere to live! We were stoked beyond words! Barb even allowed us to sign a one-year lease, which we thought was exceedingly generous seeing as my ESTA visa only permitted us to stay for three months. We assured Barb that we would soon be proud holders of working Visas, and we intended to follow through. Barb kindly told us there was a 99 cent store just up the road on Santa Monica Blvd. There we would be able to find almost everything we needed for next to nothing, like kitchenware, homegoods, cleaning products and tupperware. This was another thing I was getting used to - the cost of living in America is way lower than Australia. Really expensive healthcare, but super-cheap everything else. Go figure.

The apartment was tiny but shady, with a petite semi-private balcony, a parking space and communal washer and dryer facilities. We hit the jackpot with these digs man! It's exactly what we needed. After moving in, I continued to distract myself from the looming decision by gathering budget bits and pieces for our nest. We had not a single fork, so there was lots to do. By the time a week or so had passed, our hundred-dollar sleeper sofa was delivered and assembled. We'd grabbed a bed from the display section of Sit n' Sleep and after getting everything else set up, it was back to waiting.

Waiting. Waiting. Waiting.

An update came through: the role of Princess Eleanor was now down to me and one other girl. Huh!?!? Whoa whoa whoa. Was I actually in the running here!? I tried my best not to freak out, which was a lot easier said than done as it appeared I had a 50/50 chance here people! Holy shit! BREATHE. To avoid incessantly checking my phone, I started putting it on silent and hiding it in random drawers in the apartment. To continue distracting myself, I explored the interesting, delightfully etch neighborhood of West LA. Keep moving. Keep doing things. I spent hours in thrift stores accumulating decorative bits and bobs to place atop my freshly assembled $50 IKEA bookcase, hung out with two of my best friends who were in LA at the time and attempted desperately to remain as zen as possible.

Another update came through: apparently there were a few members of the decision-making committee who weren't entirely sold on me for the part. Aron (my agent) - God bless him - was trying to be as honest as possible while continuing to manage my expectations, as he too was at a bit of a loss to explain how little information we were getting this late in the game. Now, I know I mentioned previously that I consider myself a hustler with a skin of steel, and I still do, but this was an entirely different kettle of fish. The stakes had never been this high. That latest update sent me backwards 10 steps on the confidence train and I had decided it wasn't going to go my way. I was miserable, defeated, entirely un-zen. After having a quick tantrum by myself, I bought a burrito and a cheap bottle of plonk. I drowned my spirits in bargain-bin wine and guacamole and drunkenly slept the next eight hours away.

Waking groggily with a pesky sunbeam tickling my eyeball through the curtain, I wiped a layer of red wine sweat off my face and took a minute to pull myself together. As I stared at the ceiling, I forgave myself for last night's shenanigans, remembered who I was and the fact that it actually wasn't all over yet. A glorious new day had risen and it truly ain't ever over until the fat lady sings. In fact, the fat lady was only humming, waiting for her lyrics. I had a pounding headache, but the fat lady had yet to sing.

Checking my sugar, via trusty Glen, I was delighted by a reading of 5.5 mmol/L (99 mg/dl). Luke was nowhere to be seen, probably off for a surf for a few hours to let the beast wake on her own (smart man). I recall foggily that I had stashed my phone under my bed, rolled up in a t-shirt. I unlocked the screen and noticed a flurry of notifications. Was I seeing this correctly? Was I still drunk? There were four missed calls from my agent and five missed calls from my manager. It was 7:45am.

To ensure I wasn't losing my mind, I ran to the bathroom and splashed cold water on my face. I checked the notifications once again, they were still there.

Holy shit!

Holy holy holy holy shit. OK…………breathe. I tried to temper my excitement by convincing myself that this could also be an incredibly urgent call to tell me I just missed out, but another part of my brain was saying that it was pretty unlikely that they would put this much effort in to reject me. Oh God. Had I gotten the role?

Breathe, breathe, breathe. Have a cigarette. A cigarette always seemed like a fantastic idea in those dirty old times. Should I put some pants on? Have a shower?

I grabbed last night's Diet Coke from the fridge and a packet of Marlboro Lights. I decided the shower could wait. This was the moment. Rip off the band-aid, girlfriend, it's now or never. I waved good morning to our friendly neighbor, also on his way out for a surf, and felt thankful for the shoulder-high balcony partition shielding my bare legs and purple undies. I sat down, sucked in some toxic air, had a sip of flat coke and demanded my fingers stop shaking so that I could dial the homies back.

"Hello, I'm calling for Aron Gianinni, please. This is Alex Park returning."

Aron jumped on the phone. He asked me to hang on a minute while they connected Jeff on the line. Oh God, that confirmed it. If the news is big, all members of the team would usually jump on the phone to share the good vibes. If it was just an update, then just one of the team members would be fine. With everybody on the call, I assured myself that the deafening heart palpitations were heard only by me, that phones couldn't quite yet pick up the sounds of internal organs and that all I had to do was listen.

"Alex! We heard from casting over in London this morning. The only thing holding them back from offering you the part was that they were quite distracted by your choice of earrings." My heart sank. I began manically wracking my brain to try and figure out what this meant. Were they fucking with me? I hoped they were fucking with me. "Sorry guys - I didn't wear any earrings for my test? I haven't worn earrings in years?" I replied hopefully. "Well, you might want to go and buy yourself some earrings once you get to London!"

Those cheeky buggers!

"Alex, the job is yours...you're going to London, you got it kid."

I couldn't believe it. I felt like I was levitating. I had no pants on, it was 8:00 a.m. in the morning and I was hovering above ground like a ghost by means of some kind of supernatural power. I felt a bright warm light engulf my entire body and then I started to hear it, ever so faintly at first but then building to a powerful harmonic crescendo. The angelic, velvety vocal chords of THE fat lady herself. She was singing, which meant it was over, but this time she was singing to me. No one tells you how it's going to feel when all your dreams come true. I will say this though, the reality entirely eclipsed the dream. I guess we really can do anything we set our minds to. I could have run to Venice Beach and back, barefoot in the nude.

9

HEIGH-HO/WOHHH

About a week or so later I was on a plane to London to shoot the pilot. Typically, a production company will shoot a '*pilot*' (the first episode), then await the tick of approval from the network and studio before completing the rest of the season. They do this to avoid wasting millions of dollars on a show that may end up being a flop. Nine times out of ten, the pilot is the only episode that gets made and the show never gets seen. Networks have produced thousands of pilots over the years that never made it through. This is Hollywood, but there is always a chance it could all go away on a dime. Best not to focus on the "what ifs" - better to just focus intently on the task at hand.

I was cast as a local hire which, regardless of the fact that I couldn't be less of a London local if I tried, was the deal they offered. To be frank, I would have done the job for free, or even actually paid to do it myself. Local hire is a cost cutting method. Hiring local actors is obviously cheaper, since the production wouldn't need to pay for flights or accommodation. So I had a few days to locate a place to stay, in a city I knew nothing about, with funds that I did not have, but slap my ass and call me Jerry, was I excited.

The 10 hours from LAX to London Heathrow flew by quickly. I was met at arrivals by a unit driver called Harry. A unit driver is basically a production driver assigned to ferry everyone to and from various locations. Harry was going to be my driver for the duration of the shoot. This was cool as hell for a couple of reasons: first, I'd never had anyone wait for me with a sign at the airport before and, second, God help me if I was left to my own devices. Not too terribly long after leaving the airport, we pulled up to a suburb called Belsize Park, which would be my home for the next couple of weeks.

Harry offered to help me with my luggage, but I was far too excited to accept. I could have carried 20 bags at that point. I just wanted some time alone in my cool digs so I could acclimate to my new city and destiny. I waved Harry off and said I looked forward to seeing him tomorrow. I immediately regretted waving Harry off as I noticed the 11 flights of stairs to the apartment.

Once inside, I checked my sugar levels and discovered they were slightly lower than they needed to be. Exercise, surprisingly, can be a bit risky for Diabetics, as it can lower your blood sugar unexpectedly. I learned pretty quickly that I had to be careful while walking around London, going to the gym or climbing the stairs to my apartment. I lie on the floor for 20 minutes eating jelly beans to get my sugar up, while eagerly observing my surroundings from the safety of the floor.

I'd love to tell you that the apartment was glamorous and chic, but it was a studio with a similar layout to that of an upmarket jail cell or a bedroom on an ocean cruise for senior citizens. There was a tiny kitchenette positioned directly opposite a single bed, a small bathroom and very little storage. BUT, there was a large beautiful window that was positioned just perfectly atop the kitchen bench, so it felt a bit like having a balcony. This window gave me a terrific look-out station where I could let the breeze flow through my hair and feel exactly like Rapunzel in her tower.

I had a couple of days to get settled, which would have been the studio's idea. Frankly, I would have preferred that Harry drove me straight to the action from the airport. I just wanted to get started. Nevertheless, I decided to use the extra time to get better acquainted with London.

From the safety of my tower, I took a moment to myself before I made plans for my first day in London. I dangled my legs out the Rapunzel window at an almost dangerous angle as a means to waft the smoke of my Marlboro Light in any direction other than straight back into the apartment. I felt artistic and slightly naughty, like a wayward impressionist painter from the 1850s. In my line of sight were luscious green tree tops and Georgian-era houses with cathedral-style roofing. The sky was grey yet somewhat comforting against the distant hum of big city traffic.

I suppose now would be as good a time as any to tell you a little bit about *The Royals*, considering there's a very high chance that's what I was daydreaming about in that very moment.

As I have touched upon briefly, *The Royals* is an hour-long drama based on a fictional modern day royal family. Key characters include Queen Helena, the matriarch and mother of her three children Princes Robert, Liam and their only sister, Princess Eleanor (me!). Prince Robert is

the first born and heir to the throne. However, he is pronounced killed-in-action in the first episode. His death
thrusts his quieter, younger brother Prince Liam into the
spotlight, as he is now next in line to the throne. Liam
is dating the daughter of the help, an American (Oph-
elia) to which his mother does not approve. Their sister,
Princess Eleanor (played by yours truly), had a very close
relationship with her eldest brother, Robert, and is sent
into a further downward spiral of self destruction and
chaos upon discovering the news of his death. King Simon, like the rest of his family, is thrown into disarray
while grieving his first born son. Desperate to preserve
the status quo and keep her family under control, Queen
Helena allies herself with Simon's brother, Cyrus, to preserve their way of life at any cost. Anyway, I'll tell you
more about that later. For now, I'm off to explore my
surroundings.

Google told me it would be a 15-minute walk to the
main road where I would find some restaurants, grocery
stores, and a cinema. Feeling confident I could juggle
more than one activity while on this adventure, I decided
to see a movie and then grab some grocery items on my
way back. Phone fully charged, diabetic supplies ready in
the kit, I threw together what I imagined at the time was
the utmost chic and edgy outfit I could muster. I headed
down the 11 flights of stairs with a bubbly pep in my
step, eager to check it all out like the strong, independent
and capable woman I was.

Google maps said go right, so I plugged in my headphones, selected the best of the Beatles playlist and started cruising. *"Here Comes The Sun, And I Say...It's Alright."*
Belsize Park looked exactly how I'd expected London
to appear. The streets were lined with an assortment of

elegant looking multi-level townhouses. Some of which were pristinely maintained, others (like mine) could probably do with a paint job, among other things. From the outside, these buildings looked like they used to house entire families, very rich families I would say. Today they were mostly divided up into multiple apartments of all shapes and sizes. It was chilly out, so naturally I had rugged up in three or four more layers than were required and after about 10 minutes of walking I had worked up a sweat. I removed the surplus layers and carried them under-arm or tied round my waist like the hapless tourist I was. So much for my voguish ensemble. Oh well.

If we ever looked a bit lost, my Dad used to say "we're not lost, darling - we're just going a *different* way." I was definitely going a different way, as I'd been through five different Beatles' tracks and hadn't found the main road yet. I had to laugh at my own directional incompetence.We can't all be good at everything, folks, we must focus on our strengths to get the best of a situation. One of my strengths is talking to people, so I did just that. I hailed a postman and kindly asked if he might lend a hand and a hand he lent indeed, the sweet man. As an added positive, had I not been lost I wouldn't have had such a congenial encounter with a native Brit. The British are all so friendly.

I arrived at the cinema about 45 minutes later than I had planned. The woman at the ticket booth told me I had missed the commercials, but if I hurried I should still be able to catch the film. Feeling rather hungry after my mission, I thought it best I grab a snack to enjoy in the theater. Recalling that I now had some sort of disease that severely limited the scope of my snacking potential, I spotted a healthy frozen yogurt shop.

For the last three months or so since I was diagnosed, I had been playing it safe with my eating. That meant I stuck to proteins and vegetables. But God-damn, did a sweet healthy froyo sound enticing. The patient yogurt lady told me that they had a low-sugar option with natural sweeteners, which sounded fantastic. After checking with Glen, it seemed that I actually needed something sweet - my sugar levels were quite low. Like I've mentioned before, I found out recently (the hard way) that small amounts of exercise can screw with my levels. Even a quick walk needed to be accounted for, and it could mean that my blood sugar might suddenly crash afterwards if I hadn't been monitoring my glucose religiously.

I proceeded to purchase a small sized tub of whipped milky goodness, embellished with coconut, pecans and a few blueberries. Once inside the cinemas it became bitterly cold, so I readministered my multiple layers to account for the intense air conditioning of every cinema, ever. I took a wild stab in the dark as to how much insulin I would need to account for the froyo. I wasn't quite at professional status back then, in terms of insulin-to-glucose ratios. However, I was aware that natural sweeteners are still sweeteners at the end of the day and therefore this whole froyo decision was indeed a risky one. I figured if I accounted for a sweeter than normal treat, I should be fine.

About a third of the way through the rather disappointing film, I noticed that the screen started to appear a little brighter than it was when I first sat down and my eyes were really struggling to focus.

I assumed that when I checked my sugar I would get a super high reading - so I was surprised when Glen informed me I was at *2.5 mmol/L (45 mg/dl)*, which is breathtakingly low and quite dangerous. I needed sugar, stat. I fumbled around in my purse while my fingers started balling up and not working properly. I only had two glucose tablets left because I had already eaten the others.

Panicking in earnest now, I swooped up my belongings and ran out of the cinema. My sugar had been low before, but never this low. It was quite alarming. I should have ran to the snack bar, explained I had type 1 diabetes and needed a Coke or a lemonade immediately. Instead, I flew right past the confectionary stand, made my way out onto the street, and wracked my brain trying to figure out what to do. The lights were turning off in my head. Sugar (or glucose) is the fuel for the body. When you run out of it, your body stops working - pure and simple. As mentioned before, acute hypoglycemia (which is what I had) can cause *significant cognitive impairment*.

Fantastic. But this is my life, now, right?

I remembered I had Googled an organic grocer nearby that I planned to visit after the cinema. All I could think about was getting to that grocer. My mind was incapable of doing anything else at that point. It had locked onto the grocer as the source of food, the solution to my current dilemma, and it instructed my body to high-tail it over there. Before commencing the journey to the grocer, I checked in with Glen again and was shocked to notice I was now at *2.1 mmol/L (37 mg/dl)*. I was crying now, heart pounding like a fucking techno drum.

When a person is stimulated by a challenging situation, extra adrenaline is typically released into the bloodstream by the body. Adrenaline is a powerful hormone that can increase blood pressure, heart rate and general feelings of anxiety. This means that during a hypo, you are left feeling mentally impaired but also physically revved up, contributing to the state of panic.

If I was in my right mind I would have asked for help - but I *wasn't* in my right mind. My right mind was shutting down along with my body. After rummaging through my backpack for any hidden sugar, I found a nut bar. It wasn't going to solve all my problems (not much sugar) at this point, but it was *something* - a glimmer of hope - maybe enough hope to get me to the grocer. My hands were shaking like I'd never seen them shake before. I desperately clawed at the packet to get it open, but my fingers weren't cooperating and I dropped the nut bar on the dirty street.

The grocer can't be too far away, I thought muddily. *Siri* pointed the way and I started walking. I steamed right past an open gas station that, like the confectionary stand, would be filled with many of the sugary items I needed. I wasn't able to register this, since my brain wasn't working properly. After what felt like a lifetime, I spotted the grocer on the other side of the road. The nearest pedestrian crossing was about 200 meters further than the grocer. I was frightened I wouldn't have enough time to make it all the way up there and then back down to the grocer without passing out. My vision was getting pretty spotty by that point. I decided instead to wait for a clearing in the traffic and make a run for it. I was stranded briefly on the median strip, holding onto a pole and praying I wouldn't be collected by any of the increasingly blurry cars whizzing by on either side. I somehow made it over the remaining two lanes of the highway and climbed over a meter high fence, which badly grazed my knee, finally arriving at my destination.

The lights in the grocer were blinding. What I should have done was walk straight to the fridge, grab a juice or a soda full of sugar, drink it on the spot, and pay for it after. But I was cognitively impaired by this point, if you will remember. Instead, I stupidly selected two of the only items that would have no benefit for me at all - a bar of 80% cocoa dark chocolate and a packet of almonds. My sleepy brain was still trying to keep my actor's body looking svelte at all costs, even though it might end up killing me. A person experiencing hypoglycemia can easily be misdiagnosed as having a stroke, drug psychosis or a traumatic head injury. Given the severity of this particular hypo, I must have appeared completely strung out on drugs. The gentleman grocer and the other shoppers certainly made me feel like I was, staring and ogling and giving me the stink-eye.

I sat for a minute in the gutter outside the grocery store, desperately shovelling the food in my mouth. I tried to call Pippy, but it was 3 a.m. in Sydney, so I didn't get through. I called Luke back in LA who was out surfing and didn't answer, but called me back shortly after. He told me to go back inside immediately and get a fruit-juice. I drank the juice and cried in the gutter while he waited on the phone with me. After about 10 minutes my hands became steady again and my heart rate slowed. The juice saved my life. I got a cab home.

That day was one of the most frightening days I'd *ever* had. The invincibility coat of youth was draped around me tightly, but I was still learning the ropes of my new disease and this experience really knocked the wind out of me for a while. I was typically very comfortable going out into the world by myself, but it suddenly became very scary to be all alone in a foreign city. I needed to be more prepared in the future. I was going to be spending a lot of time on my own and I would mostly be on foot in

London. I needed to make some new friends quickly so that I would have someone to look after me if this happened again.

The pharmacies in London had a delightfully vast range of glucose tablets; the most delicious ones I had tasted yet. It was like the Cadbury Factory, but for homies with type 1. They came in all flavors and sizes. I emptied the shelves at the next pharmacy I found and promised myself that I would never run out of them again, regardless of how confident I was feeling. I was starting to become slightly concerned about how regularly I was experiencing low blood sugar. More and more it felt like it could happen at any moment and I couldn't let it catch me off guard like that in the future.

10

DON'T BLOW YOUR TRUMPET BEFORE IT'S ASSEMBLED, DARLING

The day before filming was set to start, I was informed that we would have numerous hair and makeup 'tests'. These tests involved trying a bunch of different 'looks' and taking photos of them so the creative team could get a better feel for what worked on camera and what didn't. Giddy with excitement, I was painted, plucked and pampered. They dyed my hair and added extensions, sequins, glitter and headpieces. Costumes came next, and they were elaborate and gorgeous. It took an army of extremely talented women to transform *old regular* Alex into the edgy rock 'n roll Princess Eleanor. After a full day of discussions, back and forth, trial and error, we were ready to rock and I was feeling sexy.

My first day on set was out of this world. I had been to sets before, but never at this scale. I've never seen so many crew members in one place in my life. Today's scene was set in a resplendent English manor estate. I pulled up outside in Harry's pristine Mercedes S-class and was greeted by an eager assistant director, who whisked me off to hair and makeup. There were people dragging and positioning sound-proof carpets, taping shade over certain windows and carrying camera equipment and lights carefully up and down stairs. There was a catering truck set up just outside and some cool cats were taking cigarette breaks nearby and getting to know one another over lattes and fruit juices. The energy was buzzing man. I'd never felt more alive, my whole body was giddy with delight. Luckily for me, I wasn't first up which gave me a minute to take a few deep breaths, observe the magic from the sideline and rev myself up for the moment I'd spent 23 years waiting for.

The director called cut on the scene before mine - initiating *go time*, baby. Trying to stay out of the way of the hundred-or-so hard-working crew members as they bustled about moving props and camera equipment, I stood in the doorway of Eleanor's bedroom. I was in awe. The detail was insane. It dripped with elegance, glamor and all the edge of a rock and roll princess. I couldn't believe my eyes - there was so much to take in. The art department had masterfully transformed the inside of this house into a magnificent Royal Palace.

The scene was to introduce Princess Eleanor, sprawled out on her grandiose four poster bed, dressed head to toe in black and sparkles. She was applying the finishing touches to an artwork she'd been studiously working on - an enormous union jack (UK National Flag) made entirely out of red, blue and white condom packets. Later in the scene, Eleanor is interrupted by her irritating yet lovable cousins. I mean… just sensational stuff.

The first step before rolling the cameras is to block the scene. This is an industry term that just means working out where the actors will move while delivering their lines. Then the cameras are placed in the right spots to capture the action and a number of other important things. Hatty and Lydia were the intimidatingly funny and gorgeous girls who played my cousins. The three of us were told when we should enter, how we would stand and which direction to exit so that everything was choreographed before the filming started. Once familiar with the blocking, we had a rehearsal, which is basically a run of the scene with dialogue and movement. This happens once or twice before we do an actual take.

Once we were feeling comfortable with the block and the rehearsal, it was now the assistant director's job to call final checks. This is where the hair, makeup, and costume departments were called onto set to make any last-minute adjustments. The makeup lady who was assigned to me wandered over to my bedside and commenced a last minute spruce of my hair, a lipstick top up and a blot of the skin. It was warm under the lights and my skin ate makeup at an unforgiving pace. Once makeup was happy, it was the costume department's turn. I had been cruising around in Ugg boots instead of my eight-inch stiletto costume shoes as I was told that they didn't need to go on until final checks. This was primarily to stop me from twisting my ankle or spilling coffee over the delicate hard-to-clean suede shoe. The costume lady bent down, removed my Ugg boots (as though I had no use of my own arms) and began strapping me into these psychotically sexy high-heeled boots. I have never excelled at walking in regular high heels, let alone these bad boys, but thankfully the director had not choreographed a lot of movement for me in this scene. Note to self: get some high heels from somewhere and practice walking in them.

Once the makeup, hair, and costume girls were happy, they wandered off and sat next to the monitor to keep an eye on everything. Cameras were up, lights were warm and we were ready to roll. Well, everyone else was ready to roll, but I started to get a niggling feeling...

Even though I had checked my blood sugar about 20 minutes ago and everything was fine, there was something stopping me from immersing myself entirely in the scene, an anxious thought told me I should check again. I was convinced that if I didn't check again, I would be thinking about blood sugar during the scene and all I *wanted* to think about was the *scene*. I wanted to speak up, but felt conflicted and nervous. I went back and forth, weighing up the options like a stressful tennis match inside my mind. Speak up: potentially feel embarrassed. Don't speak up: attempt the scene with a mind clogged by blood sugar concerns or worse, have a hypo during my first scene. OK yep, it's gotta happen. Just as everyone was in position and the director was about to call action, I limply raised a hand as though I was a new student at school and asked with a wimpy broken voice if I could pop out quickly. Crickets. Confused faces everywhere. "So sorry, just have to check something. It's - I have diabetes, this won't take a second, so sorry..." After I frantically explained my situation the director approached, asked if I was OK and gave me the go ahead. *Fantastic*, I thought, while dismounting the four poster bed like a disabled walrus might alight a hippo. Day one and I've already established myself as the kind of actor who waits until everyone has finished with final checks to head off and make a last minute adjustment of my own.

It gets better. From here I managed to take about four steps before rolling my fucking ankle in the Pretty

Woman boots and stacked it in front of everyone. Get it together, Alex, and pretend no one saw. Naturally, *Glen* was being an asshole, *not enough blood, try again. System error, refer to manual.* Fuckity fuck. The whirs and buzzes and pings reverberated across the silent set as everyone watched with interest. On the third go, Glen decided to cooperate and gave me a manageable, stable reading. I awkwardly apologized, made my way back to the bed and we finally shot the scene (superbly, I might add). I think it was worth it? Better not make a habit of that though.

As the hours and days of the pilot shoot went on, I struggled to differentiate every-day, non-dangerous feelings as normal sensations or symptoms related to my blood sugar. It was difficult and risky to assume that the accelerated heart rate and euphoric feeling only came from doing the thing I loved most and wasn't actually produced from high or low blood sugar. This caused me to obsess. I began checking my blood sugar any chance I could, as it was the only way to confirm which feeling was which.

Glen was never far away from me. It became my responsibility to make sure my kit was in close range for whenever I might need it. I also needed to make sure it wasn't in the shot, so it would often be hidden inside set drawers, underneath pillows or on the floor right at my feet, if we shot a close up. Over time I got crafty with my hiding spots and somehow managed to keep it out of frame most of the time.

With only 10 days to complete the episode that would determine the future existence of the show, there wasn't a lot of time to really get to know everyone. There's a certain amount of communal pressure floating through the air when everybody is new (to this production at least). That said, the energy was electrifying and I could tell almost immediately that each person was there because they wanted to be there. Almost everybody in that room had fought off long odds to be there, each small job a highly coveted position. They had all worked their butts off to win a place at the table and they wanted to prove that their contribution was worthy and essential. Like a puzzle, every piece is just as important as the next and without each piece we wouldn't have a show.

I think it's pretty safe to say that I was the youngest, least experienced, least British, most far from home and probably the most eager. I was blown away by how harmoniously, how effortlessly this group of talented strangers were able to come together, take their positions and just flow, as though we'd all done it before. But we hadn't, and it *just worked*.

I'd met most of the cast, but hadn't gotten to know any of them very well. It was heads down, bums up while shooting the pilot and it went by in a second. I didn't openly talk about my diabetes, but everyone was broadly aware. Nevertheless, I didn't have an interest in being referred to as the girl who plays the princess who has diabetes. I was still wrapping my own head around it. It was consuming enough without my feeling the need to drop the D card whenever I found myself in a conversation with someone from work.

Princess Eleanor wasn't your typical princess, as you may have gathered, which was what I loved most about her. She was a train wreck with a heart of gold. She had a drug problem, Mummy issues, trust issues, a brother who had just been killed, low self esteem and a super hot mysterious bodyguard. I felt obliged, for the first time, to share some of the anxiety induced concerns I tried so hard to keep to myself during a scene with this super hot mysterious bodyguard. His character's name was Jasper, his real name was Tom Austen. At some point, if not immediately, this guy became my best friend.

During the pilot, Tom and I shot a scene inside a limousine, obviously. My driver (I'll never get used to having a driver, by the way), Harry, dropped me off at the production location in a quaint suburban neighborhood on a sidewalk near some charming English-style cottages. It was warm and leafy there and lovely to be outside. If ever we shot a smallish scene out in public that didn't involve many characters, we did so with what's called a splinter crew or a much smaller crew. This was usually the director, cameraman, one makeup lady, the actors and a sound guy. It helped us avoid disrupting traffic or pedestrians for unreasonable lengths of time and kept us on good terms with the neighbors who kindly lent us their street for the day.

We arrived camera ready, meaning hair, makeup and costume were all completed prior to set arrival. This was time and cost-effective as we didn't have to haul the makeup trailer into a super-tight street for what would be an easily contained, quickish scene. If all went to plan, of course.

Tom was dressed in a strapping Tom Ford suit and I was in a neoprene mini dress, floor length leather trench coat and a pair of casual 8-inch Christian Louboutins. We stood curbside while enjoying a pre-scene latte and a cleansing cigarette and read over the scene a few times before we jumped in the car. I loved how low-key the vibe was while we shot on location with a splinter crew. There was less pressure and less crew waiting on us. We were also able to people-watch while we worked, which was obviously much more exciting for me than for Tom who had lived in London his whole life. I liked hanging out with Tom very much. He's a brilliant actor and I already felt like I was learning from him. He also made me laugh a lot, and that's saying something, because I like to think of myself as a connoisseur of fine humour and a good judge of a comedic bit. It's just the most rewarding and delightfully majestic thing when you meet someone you click with; someone entirely on your level. It doesn't happen often, nor should we expect it to.

As predicted, it was quite squishy inside the glamorous vehicle. Tom and I were in the back. The windows had been blackened out with cloth in sections to create the perfect lighting for the shots. There were also microphones taped into the seat-divider cup-holder thingy. Todd (our cameraman) was sardined into the passenger seat nursing his enormous camera and Tony (our lovely driver for the scene) looked the part while patiently waiting for instructions from Todd. I believe Tony may have been sporting a beret or some other kind of professional felt driving hat, which I thought was a *lovely touch*.

The way to capture a driving scene, or at least, the way *The Royals* did it, was to set a starting point (where we would start driving) and a designated driving route (often just around the block), which would lead everyone back to the starting point again. Once back there, they could assess how well the shoot went and idle safely while they made any adjustments for the next shot.

Take one went off without a hitch. Everyone did a tremendous job and I had a feeling we would finish this scene fairly quickly, which I was kinda counting on as it was getting pretty bloody warm in the limo. We were only able to use the air conditioner in intervals when sound wasn't rolling, which unfortunately was only when the we stopped at the end of the take.

Now I know I had previously promised myself (and you) that, after my last incident, my kit would never be out of reach while working. However, due to limited space, I thought it would be fine to leave Glen and the kit with the makeup girls since the plan was to stop off every 10 minutes between takes for makeup checks. We were shooting in the afternoon and the route they'd selected involved a little bit of main road traffic. It sadly became thicker with every take and progressively increased the duration of each trip around the block.

By about the fifth take, we were sitting in bumper-to-bumper traffic and I started to feel a little light-headed. We couldn't open the windows as they were taped up for lighting purposes and, to tell you the truth, I might be the only Australian person on earth that can't handle excessive heat (to be more specific, I frigging can't stand it). I'd choose The North Pole over a naked stroll through the desert every single time.

I've had a tendency to faint suddenly, since I was kid, usually either from overheating or from bright lights blasting in my eyes. Back when I was 19, on my first day of shooting *Home and Away* (the first time around), we filmed outside in the country in 90 degree weather. I wore heavy jeans and a traditional Australian hat (an Akubra). I felt a little weak in the heat, but we were in the middle of a scene and I was too nervous to speak up. Suddenly, they called action, and as soon as I started walking along the set, everything became blurry. I started losing consciousness in the middle of the take and passed out, very nearly impaling myself on an upright pitch fork.

I also passed out quite violently during a choir recital on *The Morning Show* when I was about 11. Pop Kids, a youth choir consisting of myself and around 60 other kids between 8 and 14, were singing Peter Allen's classic (I don't expect anyone apart from Australians to recognize this) I Still Call Australia Home. I was positioned at the back and started to feel a bit faint. As per usual, I was too nervous to put my hand up and ask for a break from the lights, which were hitting me hard. Just as the cameras started rolling, I gracefully fell out of frame and landed on a decorative pot plant, on *live television*. I mean - you can't write this shit. Or can you? I'd quite like to get into writing - as you can see.

Anyway, that was a slight tangent, but I want to give you a couple examples to paint a more detailed image of the person writing this book. I am and always will be somewhat of a bubble kid. I have allergies, am constantly falling over, cutting myself and fainting in public (heat or diabetes induced) is always a distinct possibility.

Back to the story. It was hot and seriously lacked air flow inside the limo. We weren't actually rolling the cameras at that particular moment, so what I should have done was request a quick blast in the face from the air conditioner. Instead, I just took some deep breaths and attempted to focus my eyes on the scene outside the window. For some reason, looking out the window actually made it worse. I tried counting landmarks as they whizzed by. Kebab shop, kebab shop, red bus, red bus, black cab. Honnnkkkk, hoooonnk.

I tried to act cool and casual while privately panicking. I became aware that I might appear quite fragile, so I made a preemptive PMS joke ("it must be my PMS - apologies") to explain this away. I wasn't 100% sure the symptoms were diabetes-related, so I tried to keep it together for the moment. I was determined to get the scene done, considering I had already "wasted" (in my mind) the team's time with my first highly embarrassing diabetes incident.

In an attempt to save some time, as the traffic had slowed us down quite a bit, Todd suggested we skip the break for makeup checks and whiz around for another take. The 10 minute takes were taking more like 25 at this point and I was really counting on a pit stop with Glen. I was going to ask for a break (I swear), but just as I mustered up the courage, Tom got there before me. "Hey, Todd, I know you wanted to keep going, but would you mind if we stop off at base camp? I just need to grab something from the girls," he said. I had a feeling his request might have been on my behalf - as, unlike me who was perspiring at an unforgiving pace, Tom's face was matte and perfect and he was as cool as a cucumber. English people (to me) seem to have a remarkable tolerance for heat, considering the fact that they only get about three weeks of sunshine a year.

We hardly knew each other at this point, but I had a feeling Tom knew I needed a break and possibly something to eat, so he played it out as though it was he who needed to stop. Once stopped, he discreetly asked the makeup girls for some cold water and a piece of fruit. Sure enough, once receiving these items, Tom put a hand on my knee and said "It's none of my business, but I thought maybe this could help. It's fucking hot in here and I couldn't help but notice you might have needed a breather." I accepted the kind assistance graciously. We sat for a few minutes with the doors open, had a drink and let our bodies cool down. Tom knew I had been diagnosed with diabetes recently but, like me, didn't know much about it. His cool-headed approach to asking for help when needed inspired me to be a bit more assertive with my own needs. It also helped me realize that it wasn't a big deal and that everyone has internal things they are dealing with.

After all that, my sugar was completely fine. It turns out I was just hot, panicking and, again, assuming the worst. I knew I'd get better at listening to what my body was telling me. But I did accept in the moment that it might take longer than expected and I can't tell you how comforting it was to realize that I'd just made a friend.

11

A MOUSE ANNOUNCEMENT

The remainder of the 10-day pilot-shoot was over before my feet hit the ground. It went by like a rocket, and it felt like one too. Now it was back to LA to wait and see if the show would be picked up for a series.

That's basically how it goes. You're a sweaty, Joe-blow hustler, driving around in a shitbox from audition to audition, loaded to the brim with crumpled head shots, a bag of clothes and 15 half-eaten nut bars. You've maybe heard about the sweet taste of dreams coming true, but you haven't yet drank from this forbidden cup.

You are a mouse on a wheel, and as dizzy as you feel, the only thing you have to do is just keep trying not to fall off. Then one day, you're on the wheel adjacent to thousands of other eager mice just like you, and there's an announcement that comes through the speakers. It's a mouse announcement, an a-mouse-ment. A couple of names are called out, neither are yours, but you know there's gotta be a couple more. You run faster. You make sure your ears are clear and ready for optimum listening, and then it happens... "Mouse number 87,465 from Australia, Alexandra Park." It's you! You pack your miniature mouse-case, you take a bunch of deep breaths and you get the hell on board the mouse rocket-ship of dreams. Once there, you have the time of your life and the reality totally eclipses the dream. Then it's over before you know it and you're promptly returned back to the mouse warehouse where you wait, back on your designated wheel until further notice. It's an intense ride.

My agents told me it could take a while to hear about the life expectancy of *The Royals*. They said that their guess was essentially as good as mine, and that this show could just as easily be picked up for a series as it could be thrown directly in the bin. Great!

I've found, and am still finding, that the only real way to avoid driving yourself utterly mad while waiting for life-altering news is to keep yourself as busy as possible. You distract yourself anyway you can.

Luckily, for me (I suppose), this would give me some time to get further acquainted with my other recent life-altering news, which was a disease that sadly didn't need approval in order to continue and presumably would be with me for life. Whether I played Princess Eleanor on the TV show of my dreams or headed back to the mouse factory for another jog on the wheel, I'd do it with type 1 diabetes, and there was still a lot I had to learn.

I had set myself up for a ferocious and lengthy waiting period and felt good about dedicating my spare time to getting to know my diabetic self, whatever that means. However, low and behold, the news came sooner than I anticipated. Just a few weeks after my return to Los Angeles, I was barely able to register the information my agents relayed over the phone. WE GOT PICKED UP FOR SEASON ONE! HOLY SHIT!

The studio and network were so thrilled with the pilot, in fact, that they ordered 10 episodes right off the bat. I guess we fucking crushed it? I was ecstatic. It was real now. The pilot we shot wasn't just going to be filed away, never to be seen again. The pilot was going to be the first of a ten-episode series that would air on actual American television sets and I had just secured my part in it!

After getting this delightful news, Luke and I planned to finish off the year, celebrate, maybe duck off to Mexico or even back home to Australia for a minute or two. Then, once it was warm enough to shoot outdoors in London without fear of frostbite and/or hypothermia, everyone would congregate back in London to shoot the remaining nine episodes of the season. I at least had a few months to get organized. I felt incredibly grateful to have received this opportunity, but also to know that I had a few months to relax and take a break from scrambling for work. What a remarkable position to have found myself in. Absolutely chuffed, I was.

Naturally, the news deserved a celebration. Two of my best friends were in LA at the time, which couldn't have been more perfect. Cariba was walking into an acting class when I called and she burst into tears when I told her the news. "I'm on my way over!" She said. "Just picking up some bubbles. I'll be there in 20! Fuck acting class!!" Romy, my other bestie, was watching a movie an hour away but, after hearing the news, she jumped in an Uber and rushed over immediately. I have pretty amazing friends, right? The best friends in the entire world. Anyway, to cut a long story short, we drank Verve out of standard IKEA water glasses, ate wheels upon wheels of discounted cheeses and laughed about how absolutely brilliant and utterly bonkers the world can be at times.

12

I WISH I HAD A SANDWICH

The next morning, I awoke with the spirit of a month-old golden retriever puppy without a care in the world. I could have drunk all the vodka in Russia last night and still wouldn't have suffered a hangover. Similar to that Vacay stamina, you know? When everything is rainbows and unicorns, the hangover doesn't really exist. I was absolutely stinging for a bacon and egg sandwich though, so I threw on some pants and made my way into the kitchen. Once there, I spotted a very hungover, minimally dressed man asleep on the couch nursing what looked to be a half-eaten sandwich. A classic indication of a fabulous night.

I quietly gathered the requisite ingredients needed for a basic bacon and egg sambo, which was a little more of an ordeal than it ought have been. It appeared that a drunk person had rummaged through the kitchen. I finally found the bread in the crockery cabinet and our cherry tomatoes were sprawled throughout the cutlery drawer. The bacon was where I left it, thank god. Cheese, being the utmost important and crucial ingredient, was nowhere to be seen. I knew I had recently purchased a shitload of cheese, specifically cheese of the sandwich kind, that I'm certain I didn't eat last night. I was determined and positive that the organic New Zealand cheddar had to be here somewhere. After searching every possible place, I finally found the cheese in the freezer, behind my insulin.

But hold the phone for a motherloving minute here, why in Pete's sake is my insulin in the freezer? Shit shit shit. Insulin can't survive in sub-zero temperatures. This I did remember. "Insulin must not be kept in a freezer, or it's cactus." was the phrase, I believe. I opened each box one by one, desperately hoping to see that one of my pens had liquid in it that still moved when I shook it. If it had frozen, it was useless. I went through all 10 of them, flipping them upside down to inspect. Frozen, frozen, frozen. Fuck, was this about to turn into another ordeal? Only time would tell.

It turns out that, Johnny, the guy on the couch, bless him, had gotten a little peckish during the wee hours of the morning and reorganized my kitchen and everything in it. The poor guy was just trying to do the exact same thing I'm trying to do right now and make a bloody sandwich. I continued my inspection, mildly hopeful that there would be even one or two surviving insulin pens. Each box held five pens and I had 10 of them. That's 50 insulin pens in total, enough to last me for about a year. All of these pens survived an international flight from Australia (insulin is simply unaffordable in America) and a risky transfer between two different fridges during the middle of summer, but sadly it was on the eve of the greatest day of my life that every last one of those bright orange pens became about as useful to me as a cup of boiling water and a ski suit on an 100 degree day.

I couldn't be too mad at Johnny, *Goosfraba*, my friends. He wasn't in his right mind and he was starving!

The moral of this somewhat pointless story is: don't hang out with morons like Johnny (**KIDDING!**). The moral of the story is: if insulin becomes frozen, it cannot be thawed, it's dead forever. Finite, gone. The freezer is a no-go for insulin. I'd even go as far as recommending a quick assessment of your fridge temperature. Particularly because if your drugs are on the lowest shelf and if you like your drinks *really cold* (like little old me), you could even get your insulin freezing in the regular ole' fridge section, and you don't want that.

Pre-diabetes, I had a very light understanding of the whole health insurance thing in America. This had to change quickly out of necessity. In Australia, we use Medicare. It's a government-based insurance system where everyone is covered. Medicare allows patients to see doctors at affordable rates. Australia additionally supports people with diabetes through The National Diabetes Services Scheme (NDSS) - an initiative of the Australian Government that commenced in 1987. The NDSS aims to enhance the capacity of people with diabetes to understand and self-manage their life with diabetes. It allows them access services, support and subsidized diabetes products. It costs nothing to be a member of the NDSS in Australia.

In the United States, however, the situation is unfortunately not quite the same. There is a very twisted medicare equivalent called the "Affordable Care Act" (ACA) which will only cover people *without* pre-existing conditions. Under the ACA, anyone who needs to regularly buy certain drugs to stay alive is basically left with two options: you can either pay for private insurance, (which for a person with a pre-existing condition can cost you upwards of $400 a month) or you simply go without. Those are the only options available in the U.S. The cost of one single insulin pen when purchased without insurance has skyrocketed to about $300 for one pen. This one pen would only last me a week and might last somebody else just a few days. The current United States health "system" is completely criminal and driven by nothing but greed, making it unaffordable for patients to access these life saving drugs and equipment. The millions of people that have been left behind by this system would probably agree with my assessment that it's a fucking nightmare.

I want to give you an idea of how different the costs are to have an *incurable hereditary illness* in Australia vs. America. Here's a breakdown of the equipment we living with type 1 absolutely *need* to buy to stay alive:

PRODUCT	COST: AUSTRALIA	COST: USA	AMOUNT NEEDED	YEARLY COST AUS VS US
BD NANO pen needles (100)	FREE	USD 100	1 every 2 months	FREE vs. USD 600
ACCU CHEK test strips (100)	USD 30	USD 200	100 per week	USD 1520 vs. USD 5200
LANTUS long acting insulin	$1.06 per pen	$305 per pen	One per month	USD 12.27 vs. USD 3660
NOVO LOG rapid insulin	$1.06 per pen	$140 per pen	One per week	USD 12.27 vs. USD 7280
Emergency GLUCAGON pen	USD 60	USD 364.50	Emergency only	USD 60 vs. USD 364.50

You can start to understand why I brought all my supplies over with me from Australia - it's daylight robbery! If you did the math, to live with type 1 in America, it costs roughly $17,104.5 per year whereas in Australia it costs just $1,604.54. That's over 10 times as much. What a shit deal! Unless you can afford private health insurance (with a pre-existing condition) in the U.S.A, the costs you see in the U.S.A column are the costs you pay. During the first three months of 2018, 28.3 million Americans of all ages were uninsured. Again, private health insurance in the U.S.A for persons with pre-existing conditions starts upwards from $400 a month, often with unrealistic deductibles. Twisted would be the understatement of the century.

So, anyways, after *The Royals* announcement party/ frozen insulin incident, I begrudgingly took a trip down to the pharmacy where I spent almost *a thousand dollars* on insulin, which would only keep me alive for just the next couple of months. I planned a trip back to Australia in late January, where I would have to buy up whatever I needed and smuggle it back.

13

A PARTICULAR WAY OF SURVIVING

After a couple of weeks of spending 23.95 hours a day thinking about the season one pickup and 0.05 hours a day thinking about diabetes, the two ideas began to morph. It occurred to me that returning to London for a five month shoot was likely going to be a much larger challenge than the 10 days it took to shoot the pilot. Five months was a long time to live alone with diabetes in a foreign land. It was a daunting feeling, but I had to assume I wasn't the only person on earth juggling a chronic disease and a new professional frontier.

I was privately (and increasingly) desperate to meet and talk to someone else who was going through the same thing. While taking this thing day-by-day, I was learning, but I knew I had a long way to go. On tough days, I found it difficult to be consoled by anyone. I truly felt that nobody in my life, regardless of how much I loved them and knew they loved me, would truly be able to understand the complexities of what I was going through. I hardly even knew how I felt, so how could I trust others to understand? 99% of my friends and family were half-way across the world and the few that were nearby knew as much about diabetes as I did before I was diagnosed.

I felt pretty conflicted when it came to participating in the type-1 community. I was aware that there were support groups available via social media. There were many others who put themselves out there, asked questions, shared experiences and, in turn, likely felt less alone. I was hesitant though - like standing next to a swimming pool, toes right up on the edge and everyone else has already jumped in. They're swimming around, it looks easy and fun, but for whatever reason I just can't seem to take the dive. To this day, I'm still not quite sure why.

I remember obsessing over celebrities who I'd heard were type 1 like singers, actors, models, and sports stars. People of similar ages, in similar industries. People who did amazing things and appeared to manage their type 1 with ease (yet weren't known for it). I was forever flirting with the idea of reaching out to any of the celebs I had discovered in my industry who were also type 1. I never did, but (and this will sound bizarre) I did receive a strange kind of comfort from simply stalking them online and reading all their articles. I craved a specific kind of support, but I didn't know what sort of support that was, or quite how to ask for it.

My incredibly thoughtful mother suggested I drive down to Santa Monica to meet with an old friend of hers who had type 1, a lady in her late 50s named Annie. It was a lovely idea, but other than sharing the experience of a broken pancreas, I didn't feel like we would have anything else in common. Even though a cup of tea with this woman was probably exactly what I needed, I started to get into my denial period. I subconsciously just wanted to avoid any conversation or interactions with other people about it. I argued that we were in completely different stages in our lives. Annie had been diagnosed when she was three, meaning she'd been adapting and dealing with it for over 40 years. She was retired, had three kids and I didn't know her from a bar of soap. I wasn't making good decisions for my self-care at this point, rather, I elected to bury my head in the sand like an ostrich.

Looking back, I guess the idea of reaching out made it all a lot more real and maybe I still wasn't ready to let it feel any more real than it already did. Diabetes already consumed my life in many ways, and I felt like talking about it to others would only encourage it to start consuming my identity. I was emotional and stubborn, but mostly just overwhelmed. I guess I was afraid of being associated with the disease more than my acting ability. I didn't want to be "that diabetic actor," I wanted to be Alex, the actor.

14

POISONED

A few weeks later, I had absconded to the local second-hand store and picked up several decorative objects.
I still have some of them today including: a rustic brass
vase, a spooky-looking mirror, a set of two miniature
paintings of colonial England and a second-hand coffee
table book about James Dean. Luke had gotten himself a
job down on Abbot Kinney Boulevard (the coolest street
in Venice), doing marketing for a surf label. Our apartment was in west LA, which was only about 20 minutes
to Venice. I dropped him off that morning, making sure
he left me the car for some frivolous afternoon activities. While nibbling on a freshly peeled orange I admired
the James Dean coffee table book that was now strategically placed alongside a couple of other impressive and
interesting books that Luke had laying around. It looked
great man. The IKEA book shelf now held the spooky
mirror in place and I'd cleverly nicked a handful of long
stemmed healthy looking shrubbery which truly brought
the whole place to life when arranged and placed in my
unique $2.00 brass vase.

I had promised to pick Luke up from work at Abbot-Kinney and I was zoning out, enjoying my last 10 minutes of couch time before I had to leave. It was about then that I started to feel a bit off. Listening to the rumble of my stomach and wiping the sweat from my brow, I convinced myself it would pass, knowing that I did have a tendency to overreact. Even as a youngster, I'd always been quick to jump to the conclusion that I was dying at the first sign of an uninvited symptom. The whole being diagnosed with an acute incurable disease thing certainly hadn't helped my hypochondriac tendencies. Keeping all of that in mind, I did unfortunately start to feel like I might throw up. I was the picture of health just 10 minutes prior and all of a sudden I didn't know what was going on. Luke called to say he'd finished early and would pick up some take away while he waited for me, but I didn't think jumping in the car right then would have been the best idea. I was feeling faint, my face was grey, something was definitely up.

After intensely throwing up for what felt like my entire life, I was able to confirm that I was in fact quite ill, perhaps above and beyond my diabetes. It was quite scary and I wasn't sure what was going on. I passed in and out of consciousness while curled up in a ball on the bathroom floor until finally I heard the door open, *thank the Lord*. Luke attempted to get me to drink some water, which sadly - God bless him for the gesture - only made it worse. I had followed the rules this time. I took insulin before eating and I wondered what I had gotten wrong, since all the food I had eaten was now staring at me from the toilet bowl. I mustered the energy to raise a hand while Luke pricked my finger. The results came in and I was right, my sugar was just below the safe zone. Knowing that my glucose tablets likely ended up in the toilet with the rest of my food and failed to counteract the insulin going to work on my already low blood sugar, I thought I'd try dissolving one slowly in my cheek. That's what Google said to do. Google also mentioned that if plan A didn't work, then plan B was to get to a hospital, immediately. Plan A didn't end up working.

It was dark out by the time Luke carried me to the car. The nearest hospital, thankfully, was only 10 minutes away. My eyes were failing me by this point and everything was getting spotty. The only way I can describe the feeling was that of low blood sugar mixed with some sort of gastro-plague invasion. It all came on at the same time though and it was this immediate, "Hey man - you've got about 15 minutes to figure this out or pass out" type of thing. I felt a sudden, excruciating fear, and unexplainable discomfort from every single organ in my body. What the fuck was going on?

Through the inside of my closed eyelids I could feel the light change from the continuous dim street lighting to what I desperately hoped were the warmer fluorescent lights of an emergency room. I couldn't get out of the car and I had this awful feeling that I was slipping away, it felt like the end. I did the only thing I could do, which was lie there and pray that whoever Luke found in the emergency room gave enough of a shit to come and help him straight away. There was somebody with him now - they began power walking. Thankfully there's nothing quite so comforting as a world-weary yet caring-looking nurse moving quickly in your direction with a wheelchair, especially while you're hanging out a car door that's mounted the curb so auspiciously in front of the emergency room.

This was the first time I was *properly* sick since being diagnosed. I mean, the first time I felt utterly *cooked*, like I might be cashing in my chips, so to speak. I hadn't been to a doctor in America, let alone a hospital, so this was very nerve-wracking. I lied on the floor, surrounded by all the other unfortunate Thursday-evening emergencies, while Luke filled out mountains of paperwork. They finally got me to a bed in the hallway and quickly hooked me up to a glucose/electrolytes drip. As soon as the needle penetrated the vein, it was as though I could feel the formula traveling from my arm, into my stomach, chest, neck, then over my other arm, down my legs, filling my toes, my fingers, my eyes. This serum seemed to instantly rejuvenate my depleted organs with a lifeline, like electricity. It was like someone turned the lights back on, one by one. I started laughing maniacally once I knew I was definitely going to survive this incident. What a trip.

We stayed there for an hour or so until the doctor gave us the final OK. In the car ride home my mind started racing with a new energy. I dreamt about the show I was about to start, I envisioned my family, my high school, the smell of my grandfather, the sound of my sister's voice. As though my spirit wanted to remind me of all the wonderful things in my life and all the mad adventures yet to come. My heart only had room to focus on the positives. I was so unbelievably grateful at that moment.

I guess the moral of this rather unglamorous recount of events is to let you know that if you're ever as sick as I was that afternoon, and you've already had your insulin, you're basically fucked and you need to get to a hospital, *stat*. The additional moral of this story is the importance of traveler's insurance. While lying there in the sterile hospital hallway, I couldn't help but ponder just how much this little Thursday evening escapade could have cost my mother. Let's see: there was the wheelchair, the bed rental, the doctor's consult, anti-nausea medication, the glucose/electrolyte drip, the curb-side parking ticket and a glass of water. I want to guess we might be looking at $20,000 dollars or so? My Mum made sure I got the insurance. Never ever leave your home country without it. Particularly if you or your loved one is type 1.

So the remaining couple of months, before I went back to shoot in London, thankfully, went off without incident. A bunch of friends from home came over to LA for a few days and we all went down to Mexico for a music festival. It might have been the diabetes or perhaps just the fact that I was getting older and wiser, but I did feel my enthusiasm for continuous partying had decreased significantly. My friends, however, had travelled a long way and hadn't recently been diagnosed with a confusing disease. They weren't planning on wasting a minute. I went at my own pace. I participated when I felt like it and had no problem relaxing on my own when I wasn't feeling up to it. I actually had bloody shingles if you can believe it, which is essentially adult chickenpox and just my brilliant luck. Looking back, I think the *shingles* were probably my immune system backfiring after my gastro nightmare. I was quickly learning that our bodies are so sensitive, so vulnerable to stress - both emotionally and physically - and this was particularly true for me.

15

A DREAM LIKE FOG

To tell you that I was excited about returning to London to shoot the first season of *The Royals* would be the greatest understatement of the century. I was beside myself. Electrified. Giddy. The studio had shouted me a surprise business class ticket, which was something I hadn't experienced before but was something I quickly realized I was very much into. While sipping a complimentary glass of chilled water from an absurdly small plastic cup, it was time to prepare for the personal preflight procedure. A procedure that is essential for me most of the time, but particularly now. I was heading to work, to *business*, which is why I was flying *business class* - because I was a *business woman*, you see. I no longer flew myself with whatever average ticket I could afford. I had been bumped up to a more luxurious status as a reward for my effort at securing a place in this up-and-coming television production. Fuck yes, we're playing with the big boys now.

Right, Step 1 - sanitation, the most crucial step of the procedure, thoroughly conducting an antibacterial wipe down of *every* touchable surface. This means tray table, head and arm rests, entire seat, remote control, cup holder and seat pocket (inside and out). I simply can't afford to pick up any kind of revolting bacterial atom - as my immune system is compromised and planes are notorious breeding grounds for all sorts of scary diseases.

Step 2 - organization of essential items; this means tissues, hand sanitizer, backup baby wipes, travel sized eye cream, rose water spray, makeup wipes, ear plugs, eye-mask, hand cream, vitamins, insulin, glucose, Glen the glucose monitor and a modest selection of healthy snacks are placed in the easily accessible, newly germ-free business-class nooks and crannies. Once everything is clean and stylishly organized, it's time to retrieve my comfy, unstylish flying outfit from my overhead baggage and make a beeline for a nearby vacant restroom. Now you're likely wondering why I wouldn't just arrive already dressed in my comfy flying outfit and save myself the trouble. Truthfully, the reason is that you never really know who you might run into at an airport. More to the point, I am a very messy eater, particularly when traveling on airplanes. There was no way I was dismounting this steel bird in a crabby tracksuit covered in chicken sauce and seaweed snack shavings. Without letting my feet touch the restroom floor, I stripped off my edgy black ensemble and slipped into my all-grey tracksuit and fresh undies. Word to the wise: travel with at least 2-3 pairs of extra socks and undies when taking long flights for freshness, peace of mind and also just something to do. (You may consider doing the same, for an elevated flying experience).

Back in my pristine pod of seats, as we call them here in the business-class section and with several minutes to spare before take off, I pulled out my laptop from the seat pocket. I decided to skim through the second episode script for likely the sixth or seventh time. I deliberately angled the screen in the direction of the incoming passengers, inviting everyone and anyone to indeed, have a sneak peak. Eat your heart out, baby. This shit is happening. No point hiding any longer. I was bursting at the seams and wanted to increase the potential possibility of a curious stranger asking about my involvement in what appeared to be an important, real and riveting television script.

I'd spent my whole life sideswiping the inevitable: "Oh - are you still doing the *acting thing*!?" type questions from irritating extended family and friends. It was repetitive, embarrassing and boring. But I wasn't boring anymore. I was en route to one of the most important and historical cities in the world to play THE princess of England, thank you very much. While scrolling through the script and discreetly scanning the faces of oncoming passengers (to see if anyone had noticed - they had not), I was interrupted by a delightful, flowery-smelling hostess named Sandy. Sandy asked me my name, gave me a menu and let me know that she would be on call for any of my needs throughout the flight.

After offering me a refreshing warm, wet towel, Sandy must have noticed my work station complete with: laptop, notepad and the pen I'd deliberately placed in the corner of my mouth for effect. She leaned over and said, "Don't let me keep you from your important business," which was stupendous as it confirmed that I really did look the part. It was official. This would be the greatest flying experience of my life. One that I can tell you, without question, has entirely destroyed my ability to enjoy a regular economy flight, which is really all I've flown since to this very day.

I had given myself a couple of days to get situated before we started work. I didn't re-book the Rapunzel tower for a second time. As satisfactory and quirky as it was the first time, I had earned a few bucks shooting the pilot and was looking for an upgrade. I would be here for about four months, so I decided separate rooms for showering, eating, sleeping and relaxing might be a little more comfortable and appropriate. I found a lovely little duplex/townhouse-looking place in a suburb called Camberwell, which I later learned is actually not, in fact, one of the most "upcoming, trendy, hip suburbs in London" as my dear friend William (Prince Liam) promised it was. Nevertheless, William stayed on an adjacent street and I had the bottom half of a stylishly furnished and modern English duplex with a rustic flare on a quiet, dead end street.

The house was owned by a friendly, very tanned English man named Tim, who lived upstairs. He offered to take me for a spin on his motorbike to see the best local supermarket, gym and doctor and all that. Remembering full well the way my mother felt about motorbikes, which is that they are likely to kill anyone who looked at one sideways, I immediately took Tim up on his offer (sorry Pippy) and we went cruising through interesting and new parts of London I hadn't seen yet. The wind blew wildly through the strands of my hair that weren't elegantly stuffed inside my helmet and my smile grew with every mile. I was like a silly puppy in a car for the first time, eyes wide open, tongue out the side and slapping in the wind, desperate to not miss a thing.

We cruised past the atmospheric Borough Market, one of the largest and oldest food and retail markets in London. It had an enormous indoor/outdoor market area, bursting at the seams with smiling Londoners. They carried bouquets of fresh flowers, cardboard boxes of fresh produce, biodegradable coffee cups and sported the most sensational selection of sunglasses I had ever seen. London was a very cool place, it was buzzing. It was chic. I was into it. Fully aware that I had taken next to no notice of the route we took to get there, I decided not to worry about finding these places again later and to instead just soak it all up. We zipped over the River Thames via the iconic Tower Bridge and I genuinely thought the excitement and adrenaline pumping through my veins along with a tiny little bit of unavoidable fear might give me a spontaneous heart attack. I held on to Tim, white-knuckled, and reminded myself that fear can often be a symptom of joy and to try to just go with the flow.

After an overwhelmingly wonderful motorbike tour of the city I was ready for bed. At least I thought I was. My body certainly felt tired but my mind, not surprisingly, had plans to keep racing until it could race no longer. There was so much to think about. At 9 p.m. it was still bright as day outside, which I wasn't used to nor did I appreciate very much. So, with no other choice but to watch the gap in the blinds grow darker, I sent a few texts to Mum back home. Then I closed my eyes and felt grateful like a yogi, which when performed properly allows no room for anxious or frustrated thoughts (do try it).

The next morning, like the first day of school, I had my backpack loaded up with all the essential nick-nacks. I laced up a fresh pair of converse hi-tops, threw on a hat and some sunnies to shield my un-made-up face and was out the door right on the dot, ready for Harry to whiz me to work. Harry said the journey from Camberwell (my place) to the studios would take about 40 minutes. That was about 30 minutes longer than William told me it would take, but I kept that to myself and made a mental note to fact check anything Willy said from here on out.

While shooting the pilot, we had no central set or studio area in which to congregate. We were essentially a group of professional nomads who moved around from location to location creating as we went. It was a lot of fun because it meant that each day work took place in an exciting, mysterious location. It's also a lot of work for the crew though, unfortunately, and it takes up a lot of time. Now that we had been greenlit and given the approval to go ahead and shoot the rest of the season, we'd been allocated a more permanent office, if you will. A studio complete with stages, a production office, costume and makeup rooms and dressing rooms dedicated entirely to our use for the duration of the production.

We pulled up to a long, winding driveway surrounded by construction sites and men in yellow vests. We were stopped two or three times by security to confirm our identities and our reason for being there, which Harry was noticeably miffed about (bless him). It wasn't until we made it through the final security gate that I was really able to see much more than a dirt road bordered by makeshift walls. Let me tell you, the anticipation was palpable. Finally, we were in and I had a clear view of what appeared to be an uncanny replica (if not the *actual*) Hogwarts School of Witchcraft and Wizardry. If you google "Three Mills Studios" and click on the image section, you will see a grandiose Georgian establishment made of century old brick and sandstone, complete with pointy gothic spires and surrounded by a murky moat of interconnected canals.

Further in support of my Hogwarts resemblance theory, ambling about the grounds were all manner of elves and fairies wearing tool-belts, transporting elaborate set-pieces, accompanying actors under umbrellas to mysterious stage entrances and communicating frantically with one another via walkie talkies.

Three Mills Studios was once the site of three huge grain mills, which is obviously where the name came from. More recently, it was a gin distillery and used to be a key supplier of the gin madness of the 17th century. After sustaining heavy damage during World War II, however, the whole urban island eventually became a hub for the London film and television industry. The Three Mills site became a dedicated center for television and film production work in the 1980s and has housed the production of many impressive films and television shows during that time. If you've still got Google up, you'll notice *The Royals* tops the list of television shows related to Three Mills (as of May 2019), which obviously suggests it's more important than anything else ever produced there... I'll just leave it at that.

I arrived at Three Mills that day, thrilled that hidden somewhere in the labyrinth of brick buildings was an utterly breathtaking, wildly realistic *Royal Palace*. Harry dropped me off and I made my way to the dressing rooms where production had left me some very generous gifts: champagne, chocolates, and a Jo Malone candle. It was the really sexy expensive one that regular people like me would never buy for themselves. Prior to my arrival I had informed production of my dietary requirements and requested that there be some readily available low-sugar snacks. They're something I've learned I need to ask for and never assume are just always going to be there. I was considerably overwhelmed to see that some kind A.D. had littered my dressing room with enough bags of nuts and seeds to survive a two week journey in the wilderness. In addition to this gesture, a bright pink post-it note said "In the A.D. office down the hall - there is a fridge, the bottom two shelves have been stocked with cheeses, meats, olives, and low sugar coconut yogurt just for you and let us know if there's anything else we can get for you."

I mean… if that doesn't make you feel loved and taken care of on the first day of a new job then I don't know what will.

From here, I made my way to the makeup truck stationed at the ground-level entrance to our dressing rooms, an arrangement I thought was cleverly strategized. It minimized the fear of actors gone "walkabout," which happens a lot and understandably is somewhat irritating and stress inducing for the dudes whose job it is to know where we all are at all times.

The makeup team had changed entirely since we shot the pilot, but I'll tell you this much for free, we were not strangers for very long. There were four or five main makeup ladies (obviously make-up men are welcome but coming across one is still a rather rare occurrence) assisted by a team of apprentices. Every time I stepped onto that truck I gained a boost of positivity, laughter and support. I had a feeling these girls would become a part of our tribe.

Actors typically spend a lot of time in the makeup truck because as much as I'd like to say that we all remain camera-ready consistently, the reality is more smudgy and sweaty. We rely on the remarkable talents of these artistic ladies to keep everything looking royal. Which requires a good hour and a half in the chair first thing in the morning, along with after-lunch touch-ups and continuity changes[1] as they present themselves.

In addition to spending a significant amount of time with the girls in the makeup truck, I'll explain the role of a makeup lady in a bit more detail. These girls are our life-lines in many ways. They do so much more than just make us look like the characters we play. A television production is like a bloody circus sometimes and actors are on and off-set all day. Everyone is running a mile a minute and it can be overwhelming. Whenever one of the lead cast members are on set they are generally followed closely by their designated makeup professional. *So you wanna get a good one*, basically. It can really help. And boy, did I get a good one, thankfully. I got the best one there is. Her name is Marie. She's a pint-sized, blond bombshell who came with a wicked laugh, impeccable early morning fashion, an excitingly intense British accent, a steady pair of hands, undeniable talent and one of the biggest hearts I'd ever seen at close range. Upon our first greeting, we were like two foreign cats, intrigued by one another's eccentricities.

Production gave Marie the heads up in regards to the whole diabetes thing. She was aware I had only recently been diagnosed and took time to ask me how I was feeling about it all. She promised to always carry a supply of glucose tablets and zip lock baggies full of mixed nuts and dried fruit and told me sternly that if ever I felt off

---

1   Continuity' is very important when producing a TV show - it refers to the effort the crew goes to to ensure something or someone random won't turn up in a scene it doesn't make sense for (like a diabetes kit in a throne room). It's also important for hairstyles, clothes etc to be consistent from scene to scene. Everything must match. If a scene upholds the standards of continuity, each shot feels as though it seamlessly flows from the previous shot, reinforcing a sense of realism in the story.

color, I must make her aware. Stern yet caring. She made it clear to me on day one that she was going to be there for me and that nothing was more important than my health. This was immensely comforting as I'd never been part of a production of this enormous scale, nor had I played a role this demanding. I was needed on lots of different sets every day, so I ran around a bit like a headless chook (chicken), which isn't a great recipe for blood sugar control. But I knew in my heart that with Marie by my side I was in a much better position than if I juggled all the balls on my own.

After Marie finished painting, plucking, combing and curling I was officially "Princess-Eleanor-ized" and decided to use the remaining 30 minutes before rehearsal for my first ever stroll through the palace. From the makeup truck to the stage doors was essentially a barren wasteland of concrete, heavy machinery, props and setpieces being painted or sawn, flocks of irritated pigeons and crew members attempting clunky first day acquaintances. By about the fifth attempt at opening this intensely complicated industrial metal door, I was about to give up. Then William, who played my brother, popped out of what appeared to be a teeny porthole-type door, within the larger, aforementioned door. It was like a peep hole, or a doggy-door, but for humans.

"Hey mate!" said William. "We just finished the first scene - we absolutely crushed it! Have you seen the sets yet?!"

"Hello mate!" I replied, "Nooooo I'm en route there right now! Which way do I go?!" He told me to go left once inside and be prepared to have my socks blown off at the amazing sets masterfully built by the design team.

After poking around like a nosey Nancy, I finally went left, as originally instructed, and all of a sudden my socks were gone. Just like he said they would be. Barefoot atop a luxurious red carpet, I found myself at the start of what appeared to be a dimly-lit hallway. I wandered my way along the red carpet and admired the subtly textured wallpaper, the strategically placed antique lantern hallway lights and life-sized gold framed portraits of important-looking old people wearing royal attire. I could hear the distant muffle through the set walls of my colleagues finishing off the scene before mine. I had a few minutes left before I was needed on camera and continued to explore the intricate sets like a mysterious cat burglar.

As I rounded the first corner, I arrived at what I had to assume was a library, the kind of library that you might imagine would exist inside a palace. It was so bloody real looking. Thousands of felt covered novels and encyclopedias in every language lined the floor-to-ceiling bookcases. They even had those cute long ladders on wheels (like in the movies) that I always assumed were just for decoration and not operational. However, to my delight I found that they were fully functional. There were two separate sitting areas, complete with gigantic leather Chesterfield couches and matching reading chairs. One faced the gorgeous Victorian cast-iron fireplace etched with drawings of nymphs and summer florals. The other was just slightly off to the side, catering perhaps to more intimate groups. With a gigantic smile on my face I took in the comforting aroma of day-old chimney smoke mixed with the scent of freshly laid hardwood floors. I traced my finger along the fully stocked library bar (a facility that, if included in modern libraries, might increase their patronage) and imagined an upcoming scene where I poured myself an amber cocktail from one of the dreamy crystal decanters before I sat down to a dramatic conversation about something royally topical.

Another of these rooms, perhaps the most fascinating yet, was the Red State Room (a term widely used in the 17th and 18th centuries). A very grand room used to accommodate and entertain distinguished guests such as monarchs, royal consorts, high-ranking aristocrats, and state officials. It was designed specifically to impress, and it certainly did. It was lavishly decorated with old and grand works of art. I'm talking big paintings, historical portraits on crack even. I mean the sheer size of some of these portraits was obscene. They must have needed a crane to get those bad boys in, each with tiny little spotlights attached to the top of the framing, ensuring optimum viewing conditions at all hours of the day. French-bronzed baccarat chandeliers glistened atop plum red velvet Chesterfields sectioned off again into three separate sitting areas this time. They all faced identical marble coffee tables, each nursing elaborate seasonal bouquets and antique silver tea-sets with charming little golden lion legs. Just. Brilliant.

Off the Red State Room were two generously-proportioned sandstone balconies that opened out to a view of the London skyline. I was utterly blown away again by the attention to detail. I took a minute to lean against the edge of balcony one, with one foot stretched out behind me as though I was Jasmine, waiting for Aladdin to land on his carpet and whisk me away for a sing in the clouds.

I truly felt like I was in a royal palace. The scale of the room was so vast it was almost intimidating and seemed the size of a football field in its entirety. This room was also pimped out from top to bottom; the art department did an outstanding job. Glamor aside, I couldn't help but shift my attention to the grid-like lighting configuration that spanned the entire ceiling surface of the stage.

Hundreds of lights, labeled by numbers, waiting to be switched on and aimed at the action. It felt like magic, to stand in an entirely realistic, breathtaking royal palace one second and then to lift the curtain and be standing in a cluttered industrial warehouse walkway complete with cleaning equipment, folding chairs, stacks of plastic water bottles, and tables covered with microphones and monitors. There was even a sweet woman wearing an apron preparing delicate canapés of miniature cucumbers and caviar for the royal guests in the scene.

Next I found myself in the adjacent Blue State Room, which had a similar aesthetic flare to that of the Red State Room, only smaller. Instead, it prioritized shades of blue as the pallet of choice. It was, funnily, a warm room, despite its cool color scheme. It was inviting, comfortable, and calming. I figured this room might be used as an erstwhile living room, though I'm almost certain the concept of a living room is just something us plebeians will understand. Royals most likely have an endless supply of rooms to live in. It would be used in the production for meetings and "royal discussions," as a place to enjoy a cup of tea and put your feet up, while instructing a palace staff-member in your most blasé tone to reach with her feather duster a little higher so she wouldn't "miss a bit."

I admired a marvellous marble chess board left in the hallway mid-game and looked distractedly for the former players. Then I overheard the commotion of crew members signaling the completion of a scene, which meant they were moving on to my first scene (hot doggy!).

"Can somebody travel Alex and Tom please, we're ready to block," murmured an assistant director. For non-film and television folk, traveling is the industry term for getting someone (who's already made up and ready to shoot) on the way to the set. Lucky for them, I was already in the building.

"No need to travel me," I said frantically through the stage walls. "I'm already on the stages and heading to Eleanor's bedroom." So that was it for my tour for the time being. All I had to do now was figure out where in this damn labyrinth they hid Eleanor's bedroom.

I ran back out into the hallway, following the direction of the commotion. That was where I needed to be. I searched through room upon room, passing by a few drifting crew members nibbling on protein bars and flipping through schedules. I figured I must not be far away when I almost had a head on collision with a flustered man carrying a 12 foot ladder who thankfully pointed me in the right direction.

Upon entering Eleanor's Bedroom, I collected my breath and began tracing every inch of my surroundings. There were shades of lucious blues and greens, pristine maple floors and walls lined with ornate golden flower relief sculptures. There was the aforementioned four-poster bed, a neat little sitting area complete with velvet upholstery, and a large glass coffee table covered with elaborate drug paraphernalia (you may remember that when we first meet Eleanor she's in the middle of a spiral of self destruction). All of this faced a fireplace dripping with candles, fairy lights and an enormous framed photograph of Kate Moss smoking a cigarette in the nude next to a foreboding life-sized oil painting of me, which was disconcerting to say the least.

Then in walked Tom. He was brooding and handsome, oozing self confidence and charisma, parting the red sea of crew members like a modern day Moses (if Moses had perfect teeth and a fantastic ass). He was dressed in another impeccable Tom Ford suit, waving friendly "hello's" to new and familiar crew members as he made his way over to where I sat on the velvet couch. It occurred to me that he was some sort of rare and exotic bird.

"Helllooooooooooo, hellllooooooooo," he said in an efficiently charming tone. "How are youuuuuu? Gooooodddd good good."

And, then, immediately after dispensing with pleasantries, we were instructed to disrobe and promptly jump into bed. We certainly weren't there to fuck spiders[2]. No time for an extra warm up; time was costly and of the essence and we were professionals, after all. So we stood up, shook hands with the director, gave each other a quick high five, removed our pants; and got ready to get down to biz-ness.

Just to give you a quick run down of the gist of the scene, Eleanor had been out partying in a swanky nightclub in Paris and gotten loaded up with a cocktail of nefarious substances. She was a disaster, a public shit show and a very lonely, scared young woman. Jasper was on duty as her newly-assigned personal bodyguard, but not without a rather dubious agenda of his own. So then, it was the next morning and somehow they ended up in bed together. Calamity and hilarity to ensue.

I'd checked my blood sugar in the Blue State Room not long ago and everything was hunky-dory, but it was the not knowing what happened *between* checks that invited the Ellis (the elephant) into the room. It was in these moments that I missed life before diabetes the most. I was 85% sure everything was fine, but all it took was the

---

2   *A commonly-used Australian phrase - "we're not here to fuck spiders" refers to not wishing to waste any time when completing ones' goal. Often used humorously and in context of drinking or partying.*

15% of diabetic related worries to make me feel like I'd left home without turning the oven off. Incredibly irritating and rather infuriating. Fuck you diabetes. Just let me do my scene.

I sat in Eleanor's cloud-like California king bed wearing nothing but a dainty red silk bra and some barely-there knickers. I picked at my nails nervously and my eyes darted back and forth. Tom picked up on my fidgeting and asked if I was ok. I mentioned that I would feel a bit more at ease if Glen was a bit closer. Tom was no fuss, and seemed to know how to deal so well with new people without getting flustered. It was like he just *decided* to do things and did them, which was so impressive to me. There are no internal arguments and sweaty moments like with me. Thanks to Tom, Marie was already en route to my bedside with Glen in hand.

"You can leave it with me, love, or you can hide it within the set. It's totally your call, and you're not holding anybody up."

I couldn't quite believe how kind they were; how after knowing these people for all of 5 minutes, I felt like I'd known them my whole life.

After checking with Glen, who gave me a manageable 6.5 mmol/L (117 mg/dl), the relief set in like cool water washing over my body.

"What's 6.5?" asked Tom.

"6.5 means I'm feeling fine!"

"Fuck yeah!" he said. "6.5 and feeling fine!!!"

Before I knew it, we were singing a song about my latest glucose reading, and we'd even begun bobbing our shoulders to the tune in a cabaret-style.

"Six point-FIVE, six point-FIVE, six point-FIVE AND FEELING FINE!!"

Tom added some lovely harmonies. We bobbed along, all while almost entirely nude in front of a room full of crew members. For some added context, we barely knew each other, I believe we had met all of three times thus far. But that didn't stop us from kicking out the jams, buck-naked in front of a bunch of unsuspecting producers. He made singing a song about my blood sugar feel somewhat normal and I was very thankful for that. In that moment without really even trying, Tom made me feel like I could just be myself and that, in turn, he would do the same. We wrapped up the first of many "singalongs with Tom and Alex" and just sat there for a minute, laughing while considering we'd likely never met anyone quite like each other before.

The scene started with Eleanor trying to steal Jasper's phone, to clear it of a video he had secretly taken of them together. This was where their character arcs began with a harmless bit of blackmail. Right before we filmed a 'take'[3] I tucked my kit under a pillow, which unfortunately was a fail. Jasper was meant to wake up halfway through my pilfering, provoking a sort of pillow-fight, which made the kit pop up right in the middle of a shot. Tom suggested I pop it in a drawer on the nightstand, so I whacked it in there.

I would've stayed all night as it didn't feel like work at all, really. It felt like a gift. It always feels like a gift. Getting there, sitting in makeup, being on set, doing the thing I loved most while I observed, and learned from others around me. I couldn't believe I actually got paid for this.

---

3   A 'take' is (probably quite obvious but I thought it would be helpful if I'd explain industry terms as they arise) an industry term for an attempt to shoot the scene. There can be only one or two takes if they're very well prepared or very lucky - but can go as high as you need. Some scenes have famously needed over 100 takes to get it right. Thankfully, that wasn't what happened today.

Once we wrapped[4] the scene, I'm almost positive I walked around and told each person I loved them, brimming with the kind benevolence of a visiting monarch. I shook hands with anyone in eyeshot, wished everyone a *splendid weekend* and congratulated everyone for their marvelous contributions to the scene. After this, I moseyed up the fire escape and back to my dressing room.

Once out of my Eleanor-attire and back to everyday Alex, I deliberately stubbed my toe on the leg of a chair and yelped like a lost kitten, as a low-fi way to make Tom aware I was in the dressing room next to his. It was a success. Tom called out, as though from the inside of the wall:

"AL?! You dressed darl?"

"Yeah! I just stubbed my bloody toe, but I'm dressed!" I replied, "Looks like we're next-door neighbours Darl!"

"I'm coming in!!" he said and, just like that, the adjoining door between our rooms swung open and stayed open for pretty much the rest of the season.

Having next-door dressing rooms wasn't planned, but it was certainly serendipitous, adjoining rooms for the two best friends. After comparing the aesthetics of each other's rooms, we agreed that Tom's was a bit better than mine as it had a bigger couch, which would be great for quiet lunches and private de-briefs. Additionally, each of the rooms on this level opened out onto a rather unglamorous steel-blue balcony, flooded with pigeons and cigarette butts. It overlooked the walkway leading to the entrance of the stage door, so that anyone who needed us downstairs could quickly just yell. My very first desig-

---

4   *'Wrapped' is a term sometimes used to announce the completion of a scene and is more commonly used to announce the completion of a shooting day, hence the familiar phrase "That's a wrap!"*

nated, full-time dressing room arrangement wasn't what I was expecting... it was far better. We had our own personal, rustic classroom penthouse in the sky.

16

TIM AND ALBERT GO FOR A BEER

Tom and I made our descent from the dressing rooms to our respective rides home, dressed in an unplanned yet *shockingly similar* attire of all black, everything (including sunglasses, backpacks and baseball caps). Tom asked me what my plans were for the weekend and, naturally, I had no plans. For whom would I have plans with? Tom was my best (only) friend in London and I wasn't close enough with anyone else in the cast to be in the "hanging outside of work" stage yet. So my plans - as they were - consisted of counting down the minutes until I was due back on set. Tom was off to "Brick Lane" to meet some friends for pints and invited me to come along. "Shit yeah, I'll come for some pints!" was my obvious response.

Tom suggested I let Harry go home early for the night and jump in the car with him. In an unlikely twist of fate, Tom's drivers' name, *Larry*, rhymed perfectly with my driver's name, *Harry*. Larry noticed our strikingly similar outfits, along with our electric chemistry and asked if we had known each other prior to this job, which immediately confirmed for me that this once in a lifetime friendship was not only apparent to me, but to the outside world as well.

Larry dropped us off at Brick Lane in East London, which was once associated with poor slums and the scene of the crime for the Jack the Ripper murders. Funnily enough it was also very close to where some of my direct ancestors lived in Shoreditch hundreds of years ago before being arrested and sent to Australia - thanks Pippy for that little nugget of information. The area itself, today, is fortunately a lot less stabby, quite the opposite in fact. It's now dotted with pristinely maintained old London pubs, restaurants, galleries, markets and festivals throughout the year. Brick Lane is extremely popular with London's edgy and artistic crowd, so we felt we'd probably come to the right place.

One of the things I loved the most about London so far was that you could drink on the streets unimpeded. Not because I'm an especially enthusiastic drinker, but because it creates a much more vibrant atmosphere. Every which way I looked I saw painfully trendy Londoners, laughing with pints of craft beer in hand, sitting on stoops outside pubs and even happily in the gutter. This was in stark contrast to Sydney, where people are not allowed to drink on the street at all, along with a host of many other very stern public drinking laws, which kind of sucked the fun out of the place. People just found a nice spot on the street, parked their butts and enjoyed the company of others, what a radical concept. The streets were lined with a backdrop of impressive, brightly-colored graffiti murals and this place was buzzing. A feast for the eyes and soul. I'd never been anywhere like it.

I learned that day that Tom had a much zippier walking pace than I did, so I skipped along behind him and took in the mouth-watering aromas of exotic cuisine that wafted through the air. This was a place for everyone, from everywhere; to be happy, to enjoy food, coffee, art and conversation.

We arrived at a street-side pub and snagged a large picnic table in the sun. "Wait here, babe, and mind the table. I'll grab us some drinks," said Tom. With a moment to myself, I whipped out some powder, discreetly blotted down my face, applied a thick coat of cherry lip gloss, refreshed myself three times with my travel-sized rose water facial spray and waited for Tom's return. Tom's friends were due to arrive within the hour so we spent every minute until then drinking beers (vodka-soda for me), chain smoking cigarettes, (because everyone in Brick Lane did) laughing, and generally just getting to know each other.

We discussed the mutual realization that our characters would be the most-loved on the show, we had tickets[5] on ourselves already by that stage. Tom had worked a hell of a lot more than me by that point and mentioned that it was actually quite rare to end up really getting along with the other actors. Essential chemistry between characters sharing a love interest was a lot easier to achieve in television when the actors already liked and admired each other.

Tom asked me about my diabetes - how it all began and how I'd been managing while jumping around from country to country. I told him the truth - that I wasn't sure just yet. I told him that some days I felt like I knew exactly what I was doing, but on other days it felt like I hadn't a clue. I hadn't had too many in-depth conversations with

5   *Having 'tickets' on yourself is an Australianism that refers to having a potentially inflated sense of one's own self-worth.*

anyone in a while about how I really felt I was managing. I guess because I wasn't entirely sure myself. It was easier to just brush over the subject and give the rehearsed "Ohhh, it's a handful, but I'm doing fine, thanks for asking," canned response and then get back to talking about something else. I suppose I avoided thinking about it or analyzing my day-to-day management as a coping mechanism. Perhaps I felt as though the more I convinced others that this thing was straight-forward, the more I would believe it was as well.

We ordered some snacks, a cheese plate, and some fresh rice-paper rolls. I figured two units should cover it. While lifting up my t-shirt and squeezing the skin above my jeans, I felt Tom's eyes glued to me as I gave myself a shot. I realized this was the first time he'd witnessed the injection procedure.

It wasn't that I felt sorry for myself whenever I saw the sad, sympathetic look from someone watching me inject, it's just that I'm an abnormally emotional person who finds it very hard not to feel sad when someone else is sad. The unnecessary emotional reaction is controllable, though, if you prepare yourself in advance. I've come up with a few tactics that work quite well. Firstly, when looking down at the needle in your belly you can say to yourself, "When you look up, whoever is sitting in front of you is likely going to look sad." If this doesn't work, a firm lip nibble tends to work quite well as a method for keeping pesky tears at bay. In particularly dire situations, if options one and two don't work , you can always just try to laugh cutely, wave your hand around and say something that provides a touch of comic relief such as, "Hahaha, oh God, I am so silly! This is ridiculous! I'm not even crying, I think I have allergies, haha!" Truth was it wasn't the act of giving myself an injection that upset me every time. It was the wordless confirmation from somebody else that what I was dealing with didn't look like much fun.

Tom asked if production had offered to set me up with a doctor over here, someone I could keep in my back pocket if ever I felt like I needed some professional support. I had pondered over the question myself, but with all the excitement of the shoot I had pushed it down the list of priorities. I would have to figure out how to buy the medications and equipment I needed while I was over here. Thankfully, since Australians are part of the Commonwealth, we are covered by the NHS, which is the public health system in England.

Tom suggested I reach out to production and explained that it was in their interest to make me feel supported. It would be hugely inconvenient if I got sick during filming (I hadn't even thought of that!). I was in a position of considerable responsibility as I played a very important part in this production. A lot of people relied on my good health in order for things to go smoothly. I was about to embark upon an incredibly demanding schedule and thanks to Tom, it felt good to know I had the option to reach out to production for help if and when things got tricky.

Tom's friends finally arrived and they were almost as cool as Tom. They made me feel like part of the gang. We had a ball and then I took my tipsy ass home where I spent the remainder of the weekend listening to rain, learning lines and generally just pinching myself. I was finding my way in this place and, in making a new friend, one that was wise and thoughtful and offered some much needed perspective, the road ahead suddenly seemed a little less uncertain.

17

SLEEP WHEN YOU'RE DEAD, THEY SAID

Not far into the shooting schedule for season one it became apparent that my experience as a series lead would be strikingly (and satisfyingly) different from my guest star days. Gone (for now at least) were the sporadic and leisurely day or two of onset action, followed by months of time off. Suddenly, I spent more of my life on set than anywhere else and with this reversal of fortune came the need for some serious adaptation. To put it plainly, I was in a continuous state of maximum exhilaration and it took some getting used to.

Most days on set were long, which was the way I liked it. On the rare half days or even rarer days off I truly just missed being at work. It was a different, more intense kind of FOMO. I was like a kid at Disneyland who'd forgotten how to slow down, or when to take a breath. Adrenaline was pumping through my veins 24 hours a day, 7 days a week and I really struggled to quiet my mind during the tiny rest breaks I *did* get. Looking back now, I wish I could have told my 24 year old self to accept and surrender to the lovely insanity of it all, to just "go with the flow."

Normally, after a day on set, cast members drop by the makeup truck to be de rigged, which was a perfunctory process made luxurious by the caring makeup girls. They would have hot towels waiting for us, take our makeup off, cleanse our faces and remove any hair extensions or eyelashes before we headed home. I'd usually skip this luxury and opt for a time saving wipe down in the car instead. Once home, I would pour myself a glass of wind-down wine and sip it in the shower. After that I changed into trackpants, cut myself a few slices of sharp English cheddar, whacked them on a cracker and lathered them in hot sauce. Then I would sit down for three minutes to enjoy my supper before laying out my clothing for the morning. Jeans, undies, t-shirt, jumper, socks, and shoes were all piled up neatly right next to my backpack which was also stuffed with fresh snacks, glucose, test strips, my script folder, and everything else I would need for the next day at work. Then, once all these boxes had been ticked, I'd inevitably start to get paranoid about not being able to sleep that night. This was pretty much the template for my evenings while shooting.

For the first couple of weeks I managed about five hours sleep after tossing and turning for the first three. Adrenaline took care of the rest and allowed me to get up and go, but as the schedule became thicker, my sleep became thinner. I remember dreading going to bed, predicting the unavoidable sound of my heart beating as though it were amplified, vibrating my entire body. I lie there in agony pushing earplugs deeper into my head as though they might miraculously shut off the internal sound of my organs as well as the external hum of the ceiling fan. It got pretty bad. I worked myself into a frenzy by double-checking my alarm was set every two hours, making sure the volume was turned up so I'd hear it and repeatedly checking my blood sugar just because. Honestly, I don't think it was even the physical lack of sleep that did the most damage, I just had no clue how to chill. There's no other way to say it. I'd brew some mildly anxious thoughts up in my head, and my hormones would turn them into a hurricane of worry.

After about the second or third week of filming, my workload really started to increase. During the last scene of the day, catering came around the set with toasted ham and cheese wraps. Wraps are my absolute favorite form of carbohydrate. I'd tried a few wraps post-diagnosis and ended up having grief each time. It turns out tortillas have the same (if not more) blood sugar spiking ingredients as bread, meaning tragically that wraps are a no-go for me.

That said, I was really hungry and hadn't had time to go grocery shopping that week. My fridge was barren and I was worried I wouldn't sleep on an empty stomach. Without thinking much further, I grabbed a wrap and decided I would just have a few bites on the way home. I really only had a few bites, I swear. But my God, let me just tell you, that wrap was utterly perfect, with a slight crisp to it, moist but not soggy, chunky English ham, salty melted cheddar and avocado. It was the most delectable thing I'd eaten in months. Sadly, my pancreas wasn't as thrilled about the wrap as my taste buds.

After showering and hopping into bed, I checked with Glen and prayed for a normal number, a number that would allow me to close my eyes and try to get some rest. Sadly, the wrap fucked me up big time. Glen gave me a devastating reading of 16 mmol/L (288 mg/dl). What I should have done was just go to sleep and deal with it in the morning (my sugar would probably even out during the night). Instead, as per usual, I freaked out and gave myself a correctional dose of insulin, made sure I had glucose and some nuts next to my bed in case it was *too much* insulin and waited it out. Predictably, watching and waiting meant that I couldn't sleep until I knew with full certainty that my blood sugar had evened out and would remain at a safe level for the duration of the night. I'd never passed out in my sleep before, but I was aware that it did happen. I told Harry, my driver, on day one that if ever I wasn't outside and ready at my designated pick up time, I might need to be checked on. If that did happen, I asked him to call me first. If he didn't get through to then ring the doorbell and bang on the window and if none of that worked, to call an ambulance quickly. I was used to living with someone; a roommate or boyfriend - anyone who could come and check on me, or whom I could yell out to for help. This was the first time (besides shooting the pilot) that I was entirely responsible for myself. I had no safety net and no additional set of eyes or hands, which added to my worries.

I was desperate to keep my anxiety in check. I attempted as best I could to surrender to the situation, trying to remind myself that my blood sugar would even out eventually. If I could just try to relax then at least I'd get some form of rest that would enable me to power through my scenes the next morning, even if it wasn't actual sleep. I lit a lemon verbena candle, popped in my headphones and listened to the essential Enya playlist. I tried not to imagine being on set, or anything to do with work as all that did was rev me up.

After almost an hour of breathing, visualization techniques and finger-pricking, my blood sugar hadn't budged at all, so I couldn't relax. This went on for about two and a half hours. I kept wondering with each passing hour how I was going to feel during my first scene in the morning. Would I even be able to remember my lines? Would I let the crew down and need a million takes per scene? The panic was a bottomless pit. My sugars finally came down with about four hours before Harry would be outside to pick me up. Theoretically this would be enough sleep. Since I only had two scenes to do, I'd probably have enough energy to bang out the two scenes before I had to promptly go home and crash in a pile of snack wrappers for the weekend. Unfortunately, my subconscious had other plans for those precious remaining hours. I couldn't stop thinking about how little time I had to sleep. I tossed and turned and started to cry. I was so angry at myself for allowing this to happen. With three hours left to sleep, I called Pippy G in Australia and wailed at her until she was finally able to calm me down.

After I hung up with Mum, I checked myself in my hallway mirror, puffy red eyes, bags for days. Marie would have her work cut out for her in a few hours. I wondered if makeup could even cover all the exhaustion and anxiety etched into my face. I mean, what normally happened in this kind of situation? Did it happen normally? Would my eyes look like this during the scene? Was I going to slur my dialogue? I finally fell asleep with an hour and a half left. My alarm went off like an icicle plunged directly into my eardrum, so I did the only thing I could. I dragged my zombie ass out of bed, had a Scottish shower (a deliberately cold shower) and headed out the door.

I arrived at work, feeling as though I had been dragged under sea by a submarine and rescued from death with seconds to spare. I attempted to keep my eyes open while Marie did her best to cover the evidence from last night's waking nightmare. Luckily, the scene we'd shoot first up featured Eleanor running into her evil uncle Cyrus in the hallway of the palace. In this instance, Cyrus has done something particularly uncool and Eleanor was furious. I believe one of the lines in the scene was "Your day of reckoning will come, you reprehensible monster!" which I delivered right up in his face, as though I was going to spit in it. It helped that I didn't have to pretend I was feeling on top of the world or in a state of tranquil bliss; that would have been a lot harder to achieve considering my state. At that point, I was only capable of expressing the truth, which was delirium, anger and chaos. I didn't speak to anyone that day at work, other than when I absolutely had to. My eyes were heavy and stinging, my body temperature was erratic and I genuinely didn't think I had ever felt worse. The director picked up on my lack of soul in between takes and asked me if I was OK. I told him that I'd had a rough night of irregular blood sugar and didn't get any sleep, but that I was fine to work. The director then kindly decided to move my final short scene for the day to the following week. Thank God, although my anxiety about how this must make me look started to flare up. I went home promptly and slept for most of the weekend. I thought long and hard about what had transpired, tried to convince myself that these things happened and that it wouldn't happen again.

As we continued to barrel through the season one shoot, I started to feel like I was on a bit of a diabetic rollercoaster. On the one hand, it felt like I belonged and that I was exactly where I was supposed to be. I was learning, growing and falling even deeper in love with it all. But, on the other hand, I wasn't sleeping and was in a constant state of denial regarding my condition. I refused to let a bad day bring me down and became dangerously accustomed to erratic blood sugar. My determination to push through the pain was distracting me from some concerning diabetic patterns. Despite convincing myself that my efforts would suffice for now, the warning signs kept coming.

In one particularly eventful scene, one might consider an emotional climax for Eleanor, it was scripted that she ran into her bedroom, slammed the door behind her and flipped her coffee table on its back in a rage and sent liquor bottles, jewelry and drug paraphernalia flying every which-way. She then reflected on the last thing her father said to her, that he was disappointed in her. Angry, confused and overwhelmed, she vents her inner turmoil by grabbing a few cans of red spray paint and "embellishing" her (presumably) expensive floor-to-ceiling length official royal portrait.

I was instructed by the director to start vandalising the room, starting with the aforementioned life-sized oil painting of Princess Eleanor. I was to start by looking deeply into the eyes of the portrait before shooting the spray paint directly into its eyes. From there I was to angrily shoot and spray the length of the wall in up, down and circular movements, however I felt I wanted to do it. Then I was to continue across the room, spraying the priceless-looking double doors and across one whole side of the room until the can ran out. There were dressers and tables against each of the walls and I was welcome to climb up onto the furniture, if my creative inclinations left me so inclined. The only thing I had to keep in mind was that we could only shoot this shot once. There were no backup walls they could wheel in once the paint had been sprayed, so we had to get it right the first time. We rehearsed several times, to angry chick music as a means to get me in the zone, and then we successfully filmed the take that you can now see in the show.

In the script, this was a highly emotional and vulnerable moment for Eleanor, she was feeling like the world could cave in around her at any moment. In order to portray those emotions, I had to work myself up into an anxious state. To do this, I would hyperventilate to get myself puffing and panting. During the final rehearsal for the spray-paint scene, I started to feel a bit shaky and out of breath. The trouble with hyperventilating is that it can feel very similar to a hypoglycaemic attack. I intellectualized the feeling away, using this thought process, as I wanted to keep going. While attempting to dismount the dresser and continue my journey along the wall, my shaky limbs betrayed me and I fell unceremoniously off the dresser and onto my ass from a reasonable height. But like a kitten who had misjudged a high-stakes leap from fridge to cupboard, I quickly got back up and scurried back to my starting position, unscathed, but rather pissed off.

Beautician technician and my personal first-aid angel, Marie ran in with Glen and the glucose at the first sign of shakiness in my arms. Naturally, she was concerned and suggested I take a short break to gather myself, but I wanted so badly to finish the scene, so I told her I was fine and shoved a few glucose tablets in my mouth quickly while she touched up my makeup. Then we shot the scene perfectly in one take. I decided to use the uncertainty of what I was feeling as fuel for my performance, which was a bit risky, but it worked. Once the scene finished and I'd successfully Jackson Pollock'ed all I could see. I checked in with Glen who confirmed that my sugar was quite low. I was alive, though, and we got the scene in the end. I was starting to get the hang of how far I could push myself in different directions. The ability to have successfully managed the illness and finished the scene at the same time made me feel very professional, despite the risk involved.

Eventually, Marie would walk onto the set to "check my makeup" at every opportunity she was allowed. She'd ask me, "How's ya *shoogs* love?" or "Show me your hands." If she ever saw my hands a bit shaky, she'd insist I check in with Glen. This was all way above her pay-grade though. They should have paid her extra for filling the position of "person keeping the Princess alive." Considering the diabetic tight-rope I insisted on walking every day, I don't think I would have made it through that first season without the love and support of friends (angels) like Marie.

Up until this point there hadn't been a lot of room for extracurricular activities. My life basically consisted of heads down/bums up, takeout, and a lot of Netflix. However, it was Friday night, we were six episodes down with four to go and there was even some kind of British public holiday on the coming Monday. So after wrapping up the long day, while getting changed out of our costumes and back into regular clothing, Tom and I had a seat on the couch and flirted with the possibility of a spontaneous night out on the town. We felt sexy and figured we'd earned it. We threw on some silky tunes, floated about to the tranquilizing fluid melodies of deep house, imagined ourselves arriving at a cliffside nightclub in Greece and instantly our tired souls were graced with a rampant second wind. We're on guys. Move out the way.

One very exciting thing about playing the role of a stylish English Princess is the opportunity to pilfer through the lifetime supply of leftover costumes to take home. These frocks and various garments were readily available in nearby trucks or production offices. It was a real treat, seeing as most of these clothes were very expensive and not something I would ever consider purchasing for myself.

I had decided that since we were about to head out, going home first for an outfit change would be a sleep inducing mistake. Therefore, some pilfering went on in order to get to the pubs while the sun was still shining. I was 92% sure the costume department would have my back: "anything but the stuff on the production rack, Al," one of the assistants had mentioned. "Just don't tell anyone and make sure you bring it back." Yes yes yes. Promise. Tom nipped down to Tescos, the local supermarket adjacent to the production office and picked up a bottle of Rose.

Fully aware of my tendency to spill a bib-full after a cocktail or two, I selected a low-key pair of ripped navy jeans, a pair of strappy (yet walkable) Jimmy Choos, a low back white tank and a black leather jacket speckled with diamantes. If I get a bit on the jacket, no biggie. A spill on the jeans may even increase their street appeal. We invited all of the costume department to join us on our escapades. After they all politely declined we cruised down the old Three Mills tower, jumped in Larry's Mercedes, chuckled at the absurdity that was our lives, called the homies, and made a beeline for Shoreditch.

God, it felt good to be out. The first stop on the crawl was a faux-historic pub that took up the whole bottom floor of an office building. There were teams of chortling Londoners sipping pints and a cool breeze blew as we rolled in. We ordered some drinks from the enormous circular marble bar positioned in the center of the room. Antique-looking swivel bar stools were dotted around the bar with little hooks for the ladies to hang their hand bags on. There were little booths too, dimly lit with individual antique lamps and the remaining few minutes of sunset peeking through stained-glass windows. With half an hour or so to spare before a few of the other girls from the show were to join us, we ordered a cheese plate. It was one of those fancy ones where you basically get a mouthful of six kinds of cheeses, three grapes and six long, crumbly crackers in a pencil tin. It's more for show than anything else I think.

Not long after, Hatty, Meritt and Lydia arrived dressed to kill, as instructed. Hatty and Lydia played Eleanor's twin cousins and always brought the party with them. Merritt is my fantastic Canadian friend, she played Liam's American girlfriend in the show. These girls became my homies instantaneously. After a couple more diabetic-friendly vodka soda and limes I noticed I was struggling a bit to keep up with the conversation. The pub had gotten much louder and filled to capacity as a makeshift dance floor formed in the center of the room. Was I experiencing low blood sugar or sensory overload? I checked my blood sugar and found that they were indeed low, which explained my disorientation. Without wanting to make a scene or steer the conversation away from Tinder dates and humiliating auditions, I decided to handle it on my own. I quietly excused myself and went to get a lemonade.

I wandered over to the marble bar and wedged my way to the front of the queue muttering "Sorry, I have type 1 diabetes, need some lemonade, sorry for pushing in." I got to the bartender, explained that I had type 1 diabetes and needed a lemonade. The bartender grabbed a glass and swiftly poured one for me, which I imagined would bring my sugar up right away since liquid always worked the fastest. Then I could get back to the table and rejoin the festivities. I drank the lemonade there at the bar and gave it a minute to work it's magic before checking my sugar again. Sadly, after finishing my lemonade I started to feel even lower than I did before; the classic symptoms came on hard and fast. My hands were shaking, my heart rate was up. I don't know if any of you have attempted to extract blood from a finger in a bustling London bar - it doesn't work quite the way you want it to. On the third attempt, I finally got a reading from Glen confirming that I had indeed dropped even further than before drinking the lemonade. Trying to think on the spot and with very few brain cells, I wondered why the lemonade hadn't done its job. How the heck could I possibly have fallen lower after drinking almost a full cup of liquid sugar? I'm panicking now as I wave my shaky arms around in an attempt to get the attention of the bartender who served me. As you know by now, if a person's blood sugar dropped to a near dangerous level, they became increasingly disoriented. I had experienced this to a much tamer degree back when I was shooting the pilot, (remember the fro yo movie disaster?), but this had to be ten times worse. My brain was struggling in a frightening new way. I finally managed to wave the bartender over and asked politely if it was, in fact, lemonade with sugar that he gave me. With a panicked look in his eyes he said "You said you are diabetic? So I gave you sugar-free lemonade?! Was that not what you were after?"

Now this is where it got weird. Instead of simply clarifying that I needed lemonade with regular sugar (which

I'm sure he would have fixed me up with right then and there), or instead of heading back to our table and telling Tom I was low and that I needed sugar right away (which he would have sorted for me immediately), I instead said "That's OK" to the bartender, pushed through the crowd towards our booth, motioned to Tom that I was leaving for a second, exited the bar and started walking down the main road. I knew I needed sugar, and fast, but I wasn't able to think practically. My foggy brain reached for the option that had always served this situation well in the past - *get to a 7/11, stat.* That's literally all my brain was capable of thinking.

I walked as fast as the not-so-walkable Jimmy Choos could take me, my brain vaguely recalled a convenience store we saw earlier. As I passed a busy train station and waited at a crosswalk, I could just make out a fluorescent 7/11 sign up ahead. I took deep breaths while continually telling myself everything would be ok as I strode past the usual concerned "Is she a junkie?" faces and finally made my way inside. Here it got even more strange as I was blinded by the comically bright lights and started to feel like I was caught in a vortex. My eyes struggled to focus on the rows of candy bars at the front of the register. I was dangerously close to losing consciousness. I knew I didn't have time to pay, I just needed to eat something. I grabbed a bag of Skittles and ripped them open with shaky hands. I managed to get a few in my mouth and the rest went flying all over the floor. The bewildered gentleman working the store asked if I was OK, to which I replied that I had diabetes before sitting down amongst the sea of Skittles and asking for a lemonade. He said yes, but unfortunately the shop owner didn't speak much English and returned to me with an actual lemon in his hand. Thanks for trying, guy, but that's useless to me right now. Still fading fast at this point, I managed to pull my phone out of my purse and weakly asked the gentleman to please "Call Tom…. He's in my recent calls." I heard Tom answer and knew he would be on his way soon. My eyes were starting to shut involuntarily now, which was a deeply frightening sign. Thankfully, a customer from the store must have overheard my muffled attempts at communication and handed me a bottle of juice, which I drank straight away, horizontal and on the floor.

After a minute or two my eyes started to clear, my brain started to reboot and I felt less fear of actually dying and more just a sense of general embarrassment. Suddenly, I realized where I was: on the floor, in an East London 7/11, slightly drunk and very almost unconscious. Gathering up the last few remaining scattered Skittles and a banana, I handed the sweet man a 20 pound note, thanked him, and headed for the door.

Back on the street, I felt mortified yet relieved. I hopped along in my stilettos and headed back in the direction I came. Realizing I wasn't quite ready to be up and at 'em just yet I grabbed a seat atop a newspaper dispenser, took a few bites of my banana and burst into tears at the sight of my best friend Tom running towards me. He put his arms around me, told me I was going to be OK, that he assumed I was out for cigarettes and that he wished I didn't leave on my own. I told him that I'd never had a low like that before and that my brain just stopped working. I told him I'd never felt such intense fear as I did at that moment and that I felt like an idiot. Tom told me I was the coolest idiot he'd ever met and reminded me that this was all still very new. We would have to come up with a system so this never happened again. I had scared the shit out of him, he said, but the most important thing was that I was OK.

I don't think I've talked too much about the aftermath of hypoglycemia (a "low"). It really depends on the severity of the drop. If you manage to catch your sugar on the way down and give yourself a boost, you can definitely bounce back. You won't have the same peak level of energy you woke up with that morning, but you can usually get back up to about 80%. In saying that, it's different for each individual. If someone has lows all the time, (like I did) the body gets used to them. It finds a way to adapt, which unfortunately results in weaker symptoms, making it harder to determine if and when you might actually be in trouble. If a person very rarely dips below the normal range, they are likely to receive the warning signs much louder and clearer because the body is used to having a healthy amount of glucose in the bloodstream and therefore even a minimal dip will set off alarm bells. When under the influence of alcohol, symptoms of oncoming hypoglycemia are much more difficult to decipher. I figured had I not been drinking, that hypo likely would have only reached a code yellow as opposed to a code black/almost dead.

It was only about 9 p.m. by the time we made it back to the pub. Of course I wanted to go back in and keep having fun with my friends, but I also felt entirely drained and like I'd just been forced to run a day long marathon while in the worst shape of my life. In addition to this, I wasn't entirely sure I'd be able to contribute anything worthwhile to the conversation after what just happened. I was angry with myself. I couldn't stop thinking about how I'd probably just shaved a good two years off my life, which I reasoned would be the effect of such physical brinkmanship after a time.

Tom put me in a black cab where I spent the ride home with my head against the window feeling sorry for myself. I sent a text to Mum, something I usually did when I felt blue. Mum was under the impression that while in London I'd managed relatively well, likely because that was what I'd told her. I chose to leave out the minor details and some of the day-to-day struggles. It wasn't until that night that I really gave myself a proper fright and it made me feel like a liar. I decided there and then that I was going to try to be more honest with myself. I didn't want to worry my mother. I couldn't imagine how hard it must have been for her.

What happened that night scared *the shit* out of me (and it's actually making me pretty sad as I write about it now). I'd convinced myself that with each setback I was learning and therefore improving, but I wasn't really learning quickly enough. Realistically, I was still in denial and it wasn't helping me be as prepared and safe as I could be. Mum suggested I should see an endocrinologist over here in London. She'd suggested it before, but usually I would feign competency and brush the suggestion off. Tonight, however, I thought she might be right. The next week, production very kindly set up an appointment for me with one of the top endocrinologists in London.

18

HARLEY STREET

Harry had come down with a cold, so Daren had the pleasure of driving me to Harley Street to see this aforementioned endocrinologist. Harley Street is in the Marleybone neighborhood of London's West End and has been well-known since the 19th century for having a large number of doctors and specialists. Kind of like a doctors row, if you will. Daren informed me that the street was named after Thomas Harley, who was the Lord Mayor of London in 1767, which I found interesting.

Daren and I departed from the studios in Bow, so we had plenty of time to chat while sitting in traffic to central London.

After briefly explaining the reason for my visit to Harley street, Daren (God bless him) felt inclined to tell me that he had recently been to see his doctor who told him he was at a significantly high risk of developing diabetes himself. He told me that his doctor said he should eat better, exercise more, cut sugar etc etc and that maybe I should do the same! This, to me, was a signal of Daren's fundamental misunderstanding of the distinction between type 1 and type 2 diabetes, a misunderstanding that could sometimes be frustrating for us type 1's.

Our condition is autoimmune and its causes and treatments are often lumped in with those of type 2 diabetics due to lack of education and general knowledge on the subject. I wasn't mad at Daren because, as I've explained before, pre diagnosis, I too, knew nothing about type 1 diabetes. The first thing that came to my mind whenever I heard the word diabetes was obesity, lack of access to a healthy lifestyle or just poor lifestyle choices. The fact is, though, a person can be living their healthiest life and still be hit with a type 1 diagnosis like a bolt of fucking lightning out of nowhere. Our lifestyle choices don't usually lead us to our disease in the same way that lifestyle choices can for those with type 2 diabetes, so it can be frustrating for us to converse with someone who talks to us as if they do. I've learned that the best thing to do when confronted with this kind of conundrum is to: A) remain calm, take a deep breath and remember that Daren is not trying to be a dick, he's genuinely trying to be helpful; B) offload an informative, serene and succinct response. I suggest preparing a few sentences in advance and keeping them in your back pocket for these encounters, as they do occur more frequently than we'd like, and are just as frustrating each time.

Daren appreciated my factual clarification and nodded along intriguingly while he sipped his jumbo sized frozen coke and munched on some extra zesty Ranch Doritos. Poor old Daren, I hope he's doing well.

We'd arrived at Harley Street and noticed the elegant townhouses with gorgeous iron balconies, vast first-floor windows and arched doorways that appeared to have been freshly painted that day. As we drove along to the south end of the street where the doctor's surgery was, the buildings morphed into exuberant Victorian and Edwardian styles with a few Tudor, Gothic-styled buildings dotted in-between. It reminded me of the Abbey Road street from the Beatles album (and the eponymous well-known recording studio).

After filling out 16 forms and peeing in a cup, I was greeted by Dr. Simon, who ushered me inside his office and introduced me to a young intern named Ralph, who with my permission hoped to sit in on the consultation. Sure, Ralph, the more the merrier. Get in, let's do this. As Dr. Simon sat behind his doctor desk, I sat on my side and Ralph kind of tucked himself away in a nearby corner, hugged his clipboard to his chest and appeared enthusiastic.

There was something different about Dr. Simon. I liked him from the get go, which surprised me. I guess I'd started to get used to fairly unfeeling, unrelatable doctors based on my experience so far. It felt like a lot of the doctors I'd met in the past looked at me as just another paycheck or another name to scribble atop their prescription pad. But, breaking with tradition, it was almost unsettling how much calmer these two professionals made me feel. Dr. Simon was an average-sized man with a bald head and a genuine smile. I guess I liked the way he didn't bulldoze me with facts and questions the moment my butt hit the seat. Dr. Simon genuinely seemed interested and took his time while attempting to respond to my concerns. He wasn't firing his answers off like memorized passages from a textbook. I liked the way he started by just asking me how my day had been. He didn't seem like he was in a rush or that he'd allocated a specific amount of time for me and the clock was ticking. I think the reason I got into the habit of putting up walls when it came to seeing doctors, was because they hadn't made me feel like I was any different to any other patient they'd seen prior and I knew the importance of treating diabetes with the highly individualistic care that it requires.

Everyone living with type 1 has different needs.

I dug through my emails and was able to find Dr. Simon's medical report from that day, I'll summarize:

I saw a very well informed young lady who developed type 1 diabetes 2 years ago. It looks as though she has been extraordinarily well controlled over the years, but she has a very busy life and has been moving between the UK and US.

She normally has a few mild hypoglycemic reactions each week which she can cope with but has been experiencing more frequent hypoglycemia recently, this includes a fairly severe episode with blood sugar levels of around 1.5 mmol/L (27 mg/dl) when she was at dinner recently.

We discussed the fact that the risks to type 1 patients with this kind of level of control include severe hypoglycemia and I have confidently told her that she is at no risk of developing microvascular complications from high blood sugar. In order to develop the severe complications that type 1's are understandably worried about, her blood sugars would have to have been at a very high level for much longer.

That was good to hear (as you might imagine). Dr. Simon told me that my "control" of my blood sugar levels was almost too good and that my average levels were similar to that of a non-diabetic. Additionally, he explained that I was probably overdoing it with the insulin because I was so paranoid of going too high and overworking my organs (taking years off my life, I reasoned), but this meant that I was having more hypos than I should be. So I seemed to be presented with two choices. Option one, I took it easy on the insulin and allowed my A1C (average blood glucose) to drift a bit higher, which according to Dr. Simon would mean less hypos. Option two, I continued to overcorrect with insulin and kept my A1C at a "next to non-diabetic number" yet had frequent, dangerous episodes of low blood sugar.

Unfortunately, even after all of his encouragement and wisdom, I walked out of Dr. Simon's office and resolved to go with option two. At the time I wasn't ready to acknowledge the gentle warnings layered into his advice. I was only hearing what I wanted to hear, which was that *I had the blood sugar of a non-diabetic*, an achievement I was desperate to preserve. In that moment I chose the illusion of "perfection" over safety and reality. My emotional reaction to high blood sugar and the pursuit of that "perfect" A1C were powerful forces. Forces that compelled me to act impulsively with insulin and blinded me to the *fact* that the most immediate danger was in *low* blood sugar, in hypoglycemia.

All it takes is one hypo at the wrong time to end everything as you know it. So, looking back, I recognize that my choice to gamble with insulin to achieve "perfection," would, in fact, be a gamble with my life.

19

GHERKINS AND PRODUCTIVITY

Before we knew it, we were filming the last scene on the schedule, bringing the greatest four months of my life, along with season one of *The Royals,* to a close. From here we would wait. We'd wait for the editors to finish cutting the episodes together, wait to hear when the show would be released and wait to hear if what we made was actually any good. Then we'd wait a bit longer to find out whether or not what we'd made was "good enough" to make some more. So I bid adieu to my Royal family, packed up my shit, high-fived Harry at the airport, and told him I'd see him soon: nothing wrong with wishful thinking.

Back in sunny Los Angeles, I spent the first few days attempting to confirm whether or not the last four months actually happened or if, in fact, I'd just woken from the most bizarre albeit thoroughly enjoyable coma. I had nowhere to be, no set time to wake up. I wasn't required in hair and makeup and there certainly weren't any diamond-embellished Christian Louboutins waiting for me in my wardrobe. So I threw on a pair of my forever faithful old converse and waited for my feet to return to the ground.

After a few good nights' sleep, a couple of trips to the grocery store, and a handful of other normal human-type activities, I started to feel more or less like a regular person again. I had started to think about my Dad.

My dad is a bloody legend. He's rudely intelligent and almost entirely dedicated to health and nutrition, in humans and also animals; he used to be a vet. Now he just tries to save the world in any way he can.

Dad taught me a lot about the importance of navigating what goes into the body from a very early age. We never had any cool shit in our lunch boxes. There were no chips, no artificial sugars, and "nothing with numbers" (meaning the numbers used to indicate artificial chemicals) he used to say. A typical school lunch made by Dad was always an adventure. The sandwich often had mis-matched bread slices from different loaves. The fillings typically included chunks of leftover dinner and there would often be contributions from several different dinners over the past month that shared a spot on the one sandwich. If you weren't lucky, you might also find any of the following on a sandwich: an entire unsliced carrot, a solitary olive with the seed still inside or a lonely gherkin that liquefied half of the bread in the hours between breakfast and lunchtime. Dad liked to take risks with his packed lunches and he didn't like to waste anything.

Looking back now, however, we know that he didn't make these lunches out of spite, as he still makes his own lunches to this criteria to this day. He always wrote us notes on the sandwich paper as well, usually in a thick colored pen saying something like LOVE U AL XX DAD, which I sadly appreciate now as I get older much more than I did at the time.

I was thinking about Dad when I got back to LA and suspected he might have a trick or two up his sleeve to help me. Up until this point I'd just sort of been winging it in terms of my diet. I had some time now and was curious to find out if there were any alternative nutritional guidelines out there that might help me get a handle on my ever fluctuating blood sugar. I probably should have asked him right at the start. Turns out he did have a few ideas. He said it might be worth looking into a version of the Keto Diet, which was something I hadn't heard of before, but sounded pretty nifty. The keto diet involved drastically reducing your intake of carbohydrates and replacing them with fat.

Now if we can remember my diabetes educator Elma, whom I first mentioned back near the start of this book. She had told me early on that there was no need for me to change my diet whatsoever. I had already decided that that was a crock of shit, since certain foods were predictably traumatic for me to eat and I certainly benefited from avoiding them altogether. Anytime I ate anything high in sugar or carbs I would experience an unholy blood sugar spike and, more often than not, an exhilarating hypoglycaemic attack to follow.

So just as a refresher - carbohydrates and sugar, which is technically a carbohydrate itself, are the food group that requires a person with type 1 to supplement with insulin. But food groups outside of the carbohydrate and sugar corner of the pyramid don't need as much, if any, insulin and can manage just fine on their own. If there was in fact a healthy way to get all the nutrients I needed via ingredients that didn't have a significant effect on my blood sugar, then this could be the strategy I'd been waiting for.

Thanks to Marky Mark (my dad), I've always eaten a very healthy diet full of good clean meats, dairy, grains, fruit and veg. What I hadn't considered yet was whether or not all these foods had a healthy effect on me now that I had type 1. I began googling the keto diet in earnest. Thousands of recipes popped up, as well as chat groups, facebook pages, tutorials - you name it. In an attempt to keep it simple, I decided to start with the basics and zoned in on the list of foods NOT included in this potentially life saving diet. Some of which I'd already cut out, but many of which I was still actively eating, including:

1. JUICE AND SODA - I've never really been a massive soda or juice fan, except for the occasional emergency DC (Diet Coke) here and there.

2. GRAINS - (barley, brown rice, corn, millet, oats, rye, and whole wheat) For me this was going to mean no corn chips, which was fairly upsetting since I quite like a tortilla chip, or seven. This also meant no porridge, no muesli, no granola, which essentially leaves me with eggs for breakfast, I guess, which is fine, but will take more effort. No rice either; no quinoa, too. Thankfully, I never cared much for sushi. Quinoa is chic as hell, but I won't cry without it.

3. PASTA and PIZZA - This. Was. A fucking gut punch. I don't even really want to talk about it.

4. CHOCOLATE AND CANDY - I stopped eating mountains of candy and chocolate when I learned in school that too much could lead to type 2 diabetes later in life. Fat lot of good that did me.

5. LEGUMES - (beans, lentils, chickpeas, beans) I was eating a lot of these bad boys from time to time and must admit I wasn't expecting them to be on the list. But, after pizza and pasta being excluded, I hardly noticed. Not having chickpeas wasn't as tragic as not having calzone.

6. BREAD/BAKED GOODS - (wraps, bagels, toast, muffins, cupcakes made from flour) Again, no shock to the system here, but still. Something about seeing it on the list did make me reminisce on the classic sprinkly finger buns my sister and I would eat on the way home from school. Also, eggs without toast were like cheese without a cracker, which leads me to the next cab off the rank:

7. CRACKERS, BISCUITS, CHIPS - I'm wondering at this point if I should just go on a liquid diet.

8. FRUIT - now FRUIT being taken away from me was almost as devastating as pizza and pasta. I grew up eating fruit on the reg' (regular). I love fruit. It's so good for you (if you have the working organs to break them down) and it tastes so wonderful.
OK now I'm depressed.

So, as miserable as I was for the first several minutes after getting myself acquainted with this intense and somewhat devastating list, I was equally intrigued and quickly began to identify a lot of the culprits I had to assume were responsible for fucking with my blood sugar. After some more solid research, head scratching and a few "ahhh" moments, it all started to make quite a lot of sense and I figured there was no harm in giving this keto diet thing a whirl.

Hereeeee we go!!! I do love a good experiment.

20

FEELIN PRETTY INTO IT

BREAKFAST

I woke up with excellent bloods: 5 mmol/L (90 mg/dl) on the dot or there about. Then I sprung out of bed and headed to the kitchen to prepare breakfast *a la keto*. In this case it was two boiled eggs, a handful of wilted spinach, and some butter.

I had been taking around three units of insulin with breakfast, which was usually porridge or muesli or something like that. Some days it was fine and my bloods would only go up a smidge after eating, but then come back down. Most days, however, I would have my insulin, eat breakfast and then, within an hour or so, my sugar would skyrocket. That led me to give myself another bit of insulin, which was more than I needed, and it would bring my blood sugar back down to a dangerously low level, putting me straight back in the shit.

I kept in mind that I wasn't eating any carbs this morning and knew I wouldn't need as much insulin. I took 1 unit only (a super low amount for me generally) ate the plate of fat and protein, and checked in with Glen every 15 minutes to see what was happening.

RESULTS: after half an hour my reading had gone down to 4 mmol/L (72 mg/dl). Perfect.

I kept checking regularly. To my delight, they actually came up a teeny bit to a 5.5 mmol/L (99 mg/dl) and they stayed there until lunch time. No spike, no dip, no worries. How about them apples!?

LUNCH

There wasn't a lot about lunch I would have to change, since lunch for me was usually a ginormous green salad with some protein, a touch of crunch (nuts or seeds usually), and a sprinkle of cheese. However, I'd never been strict with salad dressings and haven't shied away from popping a dollop of honey in there with the oil and vinegar. Luckily, I've been told I'm actually sweet enough *without* honey. I've also always had a bit of a problem with cheese and crackers, a soft spot if you will. I had been snacking on cheese and crackers fairly relentlessly for as long as I can remember. The crackers would certainly have to be axed, for now at least; another Greek tragedy.

Today, however, I began the meal at a steady stable number, ate my keto-friendly salad (kale, spinach, walnuts, tuna, parmesan cheese and a dressing of olive oil and lemon) with two units of insulin instead of three or four. After an hour or so, I noticed that nothing scary seemed to be happening at all. Had I just found the holy grail?

Later that day, I went to the gym. Full of confidence, I busted out a pretty standard workout. Then I had an earth-shattering hypo on the cross trainer after about 20 minutes and I was back to rock-bottom again. That's what this thing did though. One step forward, two steps back. One minute you felt like Mohammed Ali in the ring and then out of *fucking nowhere* someone kicked you in the face.

The reason I had a hypo was precisely the same reason I hadn't had any issues so far that morning. I simply hadn't had enough carbs in my body and it turned out I needed those carbs to create enough energy to get through all my exercises. I would to have to plan a little further ahead for physical activities now. What I should have done was either eat some kind of slow-burning carbs beforehand, or taken even less insulin with my meal to allow for a hectic workout.

DINNER

For dinner, I cooked a large piece of steak with a buttery mushroom sauce and roasted a bunch of asparagus with garlic. It was a large meal entirely free from carbohydrates. While assessing my pre-dinner insulin dose I decided to try something, something I hadn't tried before. Since I had previously found that avoiding carbohydrates meant I didn't need nearly as much insulin, I decided to see what would happen if I had my dinner without any insulin at all. I based this decision on the fact that I'd worked out that day, had not consumed any carbs whatsoever and my blood sugar had stayed at a lovely 4.8 mmol/L (86 mg/dl) all afternoon.

After finishing the steak and veggies, I waited for the results. A half an hour later they had gone up slightly -

not very much though. So far so good. After two hours, the same thing. Just before bed, I checked in with Glen for the last time. They were at 5.6 mmol/L (100 mg/dl) - which was utterly perfect and, understandably, quite mystifying.

THE NEXT MORNING

Rubbing my eyes and reaching for me' old pal Glen, I had to double take when I saw that my sugar was absolutely perfect. I'd slept soundly, like a tiny little baby without a care in the world. I didn't need to wake up needing to pee (this is exacerbated by high blood sugar) and I wasn't starving when I woke up; everything felt good. I felt normal again and inspired to see where my new freedom would take me. This wouldn't be my last brush with danger by any means, but it certainly felt like a huge step in the right direction.

21

BE SAUCY, OR GET SAUCED

Start spreading the news, I'm in the big apple, baby. In preparation for the release of *The Royals*, the network flew me out to New York City for my first ever press trip. I was a press trip virgin (as I was with basically everything else in my life at that stage) and knew very little in terms of what to expect. Thankful for the beat-by-beat "Alexandra Park Press Trip Itinerary" instruction manual I'd received from the network, I was able to locate the gentleman waiting for me at arrivals. In a matter of minutes we were enjoying a 90's J-LO playlist, puffing Marlboro Lights together out the slightly cracked windows of his snow covered bad ass Chevy, en route to the hotel specified by the itinerary.

After two hours of enchanting conversation and some impressive back street zig-zagging, we arrived at The London Hotel, on West 54th Street, just after 9 p.m. I washed the plane off my body and slipped into some complimentary hotel slippers and a fluffy robe. I decided

it was probably best I use some of my room service al-
lowance, rather than brave the unfamiliar chilly maze
of numbered streets in order to locate something to eat.
I sat on my hotel bed like the actual Queen of fucking
England herself and lathered my grilled salmon with six
bottles of fun-sized Tabasco sauce. I then sipped a glass
of red wine, in hopes that it might help simmer some of
my child-like, excitable jitters.

Sadly, the wine didn't do much in terms of inducing sleepiness, silly, really, to think that it would. Here we
were about to promote the release of season one.. AND...
we'd recently gotten some pretty spectacular news: *The
Royals* had been picked up for a second season before
the first season had even aired, which almost never happened. So, despite the fact that I was to let my hair and
makeup lady into the room at 5:45 a.m., which at the
current point in time was around five hours away, I was
in the most awake state you could possibly be. I was more
awake than if I had accidentally taken speed, wide, wide
awake in New York City.

The alarm went off about an hour after I'd managed
to slip off to sleep. I hauled my ass out of bed with 10
minutes to go before Natasha Leibel (my make-up girl)
was set to knock on my door. Feeling as you might imagine, I managed to whip my shit into gear in remarkable
time. I flung open the blinds, snatched a quick glance at
the electric pitch black , brushed my teeth in the shower
and threw my robe and slippers back on. With three minutes till go-time I even managed to smooth out the bed,
turn on a couple of lamps and got a little Bon Iver going
on the sound system, you know, for some early morning
atmosphere.

I swung open the door at 5:45 a.m. on the dot to a
very cute, slightly wet, bite-sized lady juggling two large

bags, a thermos and a folded up scooter with what appeared to be no struggle whatsoever. She was a seamless hurricane, just like me. I hadn't let too many strangers into my bedroom before the sun had even come up by this point, but I knew from the minute I laid eyes on this one that we would get along just fine.

We were allocated an hour and a half for hair, makeup and clothes, which I figured was plenty. Natasha asked me which makeup look I was after for *The Today Show*, which was first up on the schedule. I hadn't given it any thought if I was honest. My only request was that she make me look like I'd had a *bit* more sleep than I'd actually had. She asked me what I was wearing for the segment, in order to get a feel for the vibe. Sadly, an outfit was something I had not entirely planned either. To this Natasha appeared slightly surprised, but immediately took action as she asked to see what I'd brought with me. A stylist friend of mine had kindly allowed me to borrow a bunch of clothing for the press trip, but fashion has never really been my strength or priority and I misplaced the information sheet explaining what went with what.

Feeling flustered and slightly embarrassed, it occurred to me that it wasn't actually Natasha's job to choose my outfit. But there I was, stripped butt naked, throwing on various outfit combinations while asking Natasha (who I'd just met five minutes ago) what she thought I should wear.

After delicately steering me away from the jeans, boots and jacket options I brought with me aplenty, Natasha pointed out that each of these press appointments on the schedule required varying dress codes. She recommended that I *not* wear jeans for *The Today Show* in particular. How in the shit would I have known any of this if it wasn't for Natasha?! I likely would have rocked up to the Rockefeller Center and sat next to Liz Hurley (who'd probably be wearing a slim fitting pencil skirt and a delicate silk blouse) dressed in skinny jeans, a basic t-shirt and some biker boots! I would have looked like "The Fonz" if it wasn't for this tiny blonde miracle of a woman who just scootered into my hotel room! *The Today Show* had an average of five million viewers! For shit's sake!!

After carving a good 20 minutes off the allocated time Natasha had to do her job, I sat in a chair, faced a mirror and watched in a state of awe as her tiny tanned arms performed a visible miracle at a blistering pace. I couldn't help but take a moment to imagine Natasha hanging from the Sistine Chapel, filling in for Michelangelo who had fallen ill.

Natasha clued in to the fact that I was clearly going into this press operation blind as a bat and asked me if I had any breakfast, which obviously I hadn't. She said there would be food in the waiting rooms once we got to the studio, but it was usually just finger food like muffins, fruit, etc, which basically didn't help me much. I started to feel like a real numpty at this point so I gave Nastasha a nutshell rundown of my diabetic situation. To my suprise, I didn't need to go too far into detail before she initiated a pause in the conversation. She lowered her blow dryer, extended her arms as though she was in preparation for a flight, pivoted away from her station, flung her right leg up in the air and glided in one swift ballerina movement over to the hotel phone next to the bed.

"Hello? Hi! We are in room 423, we need some scrambled eggs and spinach sent up immediately, I have type 1 diabetes and this is a matter of urgency, can you have it here in 15 minutes? Yes? Great, thank you." She floated back to her equipment and got back to business. "You gotta eat, babe. Today is gonna be fuckin' nuts."

An hour and a half went by *alarmingly* quick when you were as unorganized and clueless as I was that morning. With two minutes to spare before we were scheduled to wait in the lobby, Tash (it felt natural to switch to a nickname by this point) had packed and strapped her loot up to her tiny body once again and was ushering my 96% dressed ass out the door. Earrings and shoes went on in the elevator. BING, doors flung open. Sunglasses went on in an unplanned yet entirely synchronized right hand swoop as we glided out to the car like Batman and Robin, right on time and looking chic as hell. New York City, *The Today Show*, five million viewers, let's do this shit.

Soon after arriving at the green room[6] we were mic'd up[7] and reunited with my on-screen brother William, who was hovering around the snack table. As predicted, the snack table was an elaborate display of carbs and sugar-heavy treats, all of which I would have regretted consuming for the entire day had it not been for Tiny Tash.

Elizabeth referred to my outfit as enchanting, after which I gave a silent thumbs-up to Tash in the back. Before I had a second to realize what the hell was even happening, we were escorted backstage. I felt instantly sweaty and accepted a tissue for my armpits from Tash. I focused on following the long, stable strides of Elizabeth, who had walked in heels - let's just say - a few more times

---

6   The 'Green Room' is a term used to describe the main room where performers congregate backstage before going onstage. It usually has green carpet or a green theme. It's a tradition.

7   Getting 'mic'd up' refers to having your microphone attached to your hip with the receiver on your lapel, so that the audience will hear everything I say.

than I had, while breathing through the possibility that I might have been experiencing a pre-live-television mini panic attack.

We walked in single file down the corridors, which bustled with frantic people wearing headsets and carrying clipboards. I wracked my brain for any interesting facts about *The Royals* I might be able to whip out during the interview. They gave us a page of talking points, but as soon as we were jostled to set my mind went blank of any useful facts. My brain felt as though it might shut down completely, leaving an empty, black screen. I knew I was on a show called *The Royals* and that I played Princess Eleanor, but that was quite literally it.

I pivoted around to Tiny Tash for some moral support and mouthed the words "I'm fucked. I've got no idea what to say if they ask me anything." Tash giggled and mouthed, "you'll be fine." Before I had time for further argument, we reached the end of the line and stood behind a thin curtain, getting ready to stroll on-camera. The curtain was slightly see-through and I saw a bunch of cameras, several busy crew members, two ladies sitting on couches and what looked like a live audience of a couple hundred people.

Kathy Lee and Hoda (the two exquisite hosts of *Today Show*) finished up the segment they were on, something about a special ice sculptor, and then I heard the entrance music, which meant that they were introducing us and we were about to go live. I felt like I could have passed out at any moment, which reminded me, concerningly, that I hadn't checked in with Glen since we left the hotel. Fuck, fuck, fuck. I swivelled back to Tash for my last "phone a friend" moment and I didn't even need to say anything. The look on my face must have been enough.

She said "It's OK, I have it here, we have time." She whipped Glen out of her bag and asked me to breathe in order to steady my fingers. I was at 4.1 mmol/L (73 mg/dl), not too bad but a bit on the lower end. She pulled out some glucose tablets, I threw a couple in my mouth and chewed them as I followed Elizabeth onto the set. I spotted Tash peeking through the curtain and was able to identify the shift in my thumping heart had gone from panic to excitement. I was secure in the knowledge that I was now very unlikely to pass out on-camera, thanks to the two preemptive glucose tablets I just scoffed. With great relief and my confidence reborn, I glided over to the orange couch next to E. Hurley and arranged my legs in the elegant-yet-professional configuration she had kindly demonstrated for me some time ago back on set. I also copied her waving and smiling and focused deeply on recounting searingly witty one-liners about *The Royals* if and when the opportunity to speak presented itself.

Elizabeth took the reins, thank Christ. Dripping with confidence. These sorts of interviews were like collecting the milk for E. Hurley. When Kathy Lee occasionally sent a question in my direction, Elizabeth would almost answer it for me first, started me off with a sentence or two and allowed me to simply agree or elaborate on her point. This made everything so, so much easier. It was a tremendous system that allowed me a few seconds to rearrange the disoriented jargon that likely would have come out had I just answered on my own. Praise Be E. Hurley.

A five minute segment on live TV passes by in the blink of an eye, a fact that I'll endeavour to remember next time. By the time everybody said hello and we viewed a couple of clips, there was really only time for a handful of questions and answers. The on-camera interview went swimmingly since everybody else knew exactly what they were doing. I had also worked out a system for if the question I was asked wasn't one I immediately knew how to answer. I would politely turn my head towards Liz or William and invited them to chime in, which *hopefully* would have just made me look cute and polite as opposed to anything negative. You know?!

'Twas a long day. We were allocated time for lunch, but we also needed to hot-foot it across town for some more interviews and the traffic was stupendously bad. So we sort of just ate in the car while we circled the block a few times. Most of my on-camera interviews involved Elizabeth and William, but the one right after lunch was just me on my own. The anxiety crept back fairly heavily prior to my first solo interview, as well as the fact that I would be alone and responsible for the majority of the conversation points. I had also just taken insulin, eaten lunch, and was anxiously waiting to find out if anything bad was going to happen or if I would get delirious again.

The new low carb diet was going great in terms of limiting post meal spikes, but it did make me feel like I was skating on thin ice in terms of going low. I was struggling to trust that I'd given myself the correct dosage and that I wasn't going to crash, which meant I was checking my blood glucose up to 30 times a day. Even when I got a healthy reading back from Glen, I was in constant fear that the reading could change any minute. It was really difficult not to obsess over that possibility.

Tash said I did great, which I appreciated, as it certainly didn't feel like my bubbliest appearance. I focused on the interviewer, on every word she said, and forced the looming anxiety to the side. I reminded myself that it would be over soon, that most likely I was fine, and that I could check with Glen as soon as they cut the cameras.

The press trip was absolutely bonkers. Last up on the weekend schedule, we were to attend a thing called the Upfronts, which are annual presentations where the TV networks reveal their fall line-ups to advertisers and press. Basically, the networks fly out a handful of cast members from each of their shows, dress them up and parade them around so the big guys can decide where they want to spend their advertising dollars.

Tash was due to arrive for another beautification process in 30 minutes, so I rolled out of bed, took an ice cold shower, hurriedly threw on a very strange outfit (complete with an awkward beanie covering my wet hair) and went downstairs to grab some coffee. I was naive to think this would be a slick and covert operation, as unfortunately the elevator stopped at level 12 where I was joined by the complete and actual J-LO (Jennifer Lopez, of all fucking people) who rode with me to the lobby. After grabbing the coffees I had a cigarette in what I believed was a discrete alleyway and tried to figure out how on earth I'd ended up staying in the same hotel as J-LO.

Back in the safety of my room, Tash told me the reason we were all together in the same hotel. The network would have scored a block rate on the rooms for their talent and it also made it easy for paparazzi to secure choreographed shots of us all leaving for the event pre-windswept and looking glamorous. Good. OK. Will jot that down in my "book of things to remember for next time." It was just completely fascinating, the thought that clearly went into the whole ordeal.

After Tash was done transforming me from a drowned rat to someone who *almost* looked like they belonged at these types of events, we met Elizabeth and William in the lobby at the designated cast members time-slot. There we met with our publicist, Patrick, who was running us through the hotel-to-car exit strategy. Unfortunately, I wasn't listening and before there was time to ask anyone what was happening, Elizabeth made pace for the exit. I looked around for Tash who was nowhere to be seen and figured I would just do what I usually did and follow Elizabeth. The doors swung open to a sea of men in black holding blinding, flashing cameras. I looked back in search of William, who was not in fact behind me like I'd hoped, but stationary inside the hotel with a very pleased grin on his face. The face said it all: "You've gone too soon mate." *Christ*! Elizabeth doesn't need or want an escort on the red carpet! I was supposed to hang back and wait for Elizabeth to excite the press, *then* walk out with William, which I am now positive was the instruction clearly given just moments ago by Patrick the publicist. Great. Fucking spectacular. Feeling like a deer caught in headlights, I calculated that it would be much much worse to turn back now. Focusing on remaining perpendicular to the ground, I continued to trail Elizabeth to her car, which obviously was loaded with her entourage and had no room for me. It wasn't until Elizabeth was seated in the vehicle that she was made aware of my unplanned arrival, but before I knew it I was sitting on the lap of a man named Bradley and we were on our way.

Once reunited with the rest of the gang, we walked the red carpet and headed backstage where I went in search of a quiet corner to catch my breath. Before I had a chance to count back from three, I found myself instructing the entire Kardashian family on where the bathrooms were. Just politely say you don't know, Alex, if you don't know, don't pretend that you know, you don't have to know, now we're all just standing here confused and uncomfortable. Anyway, in a nutshell, the 'upfronts' are basically a bizarre circus-type event where anyone from the international powerhouse (that is J-LO, to the Kardashian family) to me, Willy and Elizabeth are allocated a slot in which to stand on a big stage and twirl around in a circle while an audience of businessy looking people take notes and discuss. Weird. Lovely! But mostly pretty fucking weird.

I made it back to my hotel room, finally, after what felt like an extended acid trip. I must have passed out immediately as, when I woke, it was dark out, my left eye was glued shut, and I was still wearing shoes. I followed the vibrations of my phone and found it wedged between the mattress and the headboard. I was delighted to receive a plethora of text messages from Tom who had kindly sent links to the paparazzi photos of us leaving the hotel along with 16 crying with laughter emojis. There were pictures of Elizabeth heading to Upfronts, looking exactly as you'd expect, tall, confident, ravishing; and, hang on…there I am, there's Al! Head down, staring at her feet, hair all over her face, arms in the air waving about like she's hailing a cab in the rain. Amazing. My first ever paparazzi photos ever and I look like Wednesday Adams has turned up on the red carpet ready for a photo-bomb. Why was I waving!? Elizabeth wasn't waving! She's just walking and smiling with her head up like she's got somewhere to fucking be! It's fine, it was good while it lasted. I'll await the employment termination email under the safety of this duvet. A good evening to all. Adieu to yer, and yer, and yer.

Next up on *The Royals* agenda we were headed to Cannes, France, for an event known as MIPCOM, which is an entertainment content market. It's similar to Upfronts, but a bit bigger and included more international shows (if you can even believe they decided to send me there). It was a quick detour before we headed back to London to start filming season two.

Anyway, this will be quick, it's mostly just too rad not to share. It was one of the last times in a long while that for whatever reason, my diabetes decided to chill the F out and let me just be a free spirited baller for a minute. Cannes was a fairly regular stomping ground for Elizabeth, who I believe had just zipped over on her private jet. William and I weren't invited to join, which was fine, we could handle it! We were confident. We could manage without our travel and press savvy onscreen mother. Our luggage was held up or on another flight or something - but that didn't concern us, rather it was quite convenient as it freed us up for an immediate search for something to eat. We asked the driver to let us out right in the centre of the action, assuring him we had the brain power to find the hotel on our own without his needing to wait for us. I suspected this could be a mistake, but we were far too enchanted to resist.

We skipped through the breathtakingly sexy town of Cannes like a couple of kids gone rogue on a school excursion. We peeked in the windows of designer stores, admired the glistening Mediterranean sea, spotted with hundred-million-dollar yachts and packed with people so glamorous I couldn't help but wonder if we had walked onto the set of a Bond film. I didn't see a single shit car and wondered if perhaps they were banned in Cannes. The taxis were Mercedes, the buildings were sandstone, antique, but pristinely preserved. This place was flawless, not a single piece of rubbish on the ground. I didn't see one person of any age who didn't appear as though they had just walked off a high-end photo shoot. Naturally, this made me feel increasingly inadequate in my plane-food-stained jeans, torn red hoodie and Royals season one backpack. To make matters worse, Willy was unfortunately, *yet unsurprisingly* dressed identical to me. Determined to find some food, we figured there had to be a low key alternative to the vast array of high end establishments we had passed thus far. Hopefully a place without an implied dress code and ideally a place that we wouldn't be expected to pay 70 euros for a chicken salad, which appeared to be the going rate here in fucking Cannes! But William was resolved to only pay London rates at the very maximum, since London was expensive enough (I think you'll all agree).

"William, this is just how it is here. We've been walking around for an hour, I'm getting very sweaty, and I'll probably have a hypo soon…" I wasn't going to have a hypo. I was just frustrated by William's stubborn prudence and forever level headed thinking even during times of starvation in foreign countries. "Let's just pay the 70 fucking euros and go in for fuck's sake." William wasn't having any of it though. He wouldn't admit defeat just yet. In the meantime, I parked my butt on a nearby bench and got to work on an emergency nut bar while William carried on Googling for "subway sandwiches near me."

After ripping open the packet, a seagull flew over my head, scared the shit out of me and took off with my nut bar. Right as I was about to reach my breaking point, a dog-walker dressed in a pin-striped silk suit approached.

We attempted to converse, but spoke different languages. Getting nowhere fast, we did the thing where two foreign strangers attempt to communicate via sputters of gibberish, long pauses, and squinted eyes before she reverted to the universally-accepted technique of pointing wildly. I complied to the best of my ability, assuming she must have been asking for directions, or had perhaps mistaken me for another disheveled tourist. I swung around and followed her finger, which at first glance appeared to be pointed directly at a standard large tree. Struggling to catch on, I used hand gestures and a facial expression that implicated my confusion. The pointing grew wilder, aggressive almost. I prevailed, searched beyond the tree and to my absolute horror and delight my eyes landed on an enormous image of a face that I was 90% sure was in fact mine. I pivoted around for a clearer vantage point and it was undeniable. I wasn't mistaken. I was staring at an enormous poster hanging the entire length of the Intercontinental Carlton (one of the most famous hotels in Cannes, in all the movies, Google it, you'll recognize it) with my face on it. Willy's face was there too; he was on the next poster over. Thanking the friendly stranger via a high five and a giggle, I yelled down to William who was waving his phone around by the shoreline, presumably in pursuit of a stronger signal. He ignored me at first, but then ran over to where I was standing and promptly claimed that he'd discovered the baffling images first (which is an absolute classic Willy move).

After staring blankly in a prolonged silence at the posters, and then back at each other, we discreetly took some photos of us looking casual in front of our posters and sent them to our Mums. We then thought "fuck it," and proceeded to the nearest snazzy restaurant, where we sat confidently in our post-flight filth and devoured a couple of tiny 60 Euro salads.

My blood sugar was completely fine during our 48 hours in Cannes, since I stuck to the new low-carb diet. I even took one tiny bite out of the complimentary tray of macaroons that were waiting in my hotel room and gave the rest to Willy without even feeling slightly sorry for myself. How on earth could one feel sorry for themselves during a free trip to Cannes? Macaroons or no Macaroons, I was far too *dazzled* to let diabetes take up a second more of my time than it needed to.

The MIPCOM event itself was swift. Elizabeth stood at the end of a jetty looking monumental in a knee-length crimson number, and William took his position to her left, dazzling his legions of Narnia fans without a care in the world. Then there was me to the right, a couple of inches *deliberately* behind Elizabeth this time, (see, at least I learned from the NYC photo bomb offense) strapped into another pair of shoes I could barely stand in, breathing deeply and wondering what was for dinner.

Elizabeth had invited William and myself to join her for dinner, which I was thrilled with because going anywhere with Elizabeth was always exciting for obvious reasons. Elizabeth is incredibly famous, a spotlight surrounds her wherever she goes. Lucky for me, the spotlight only covers Elizabeth exclusively, leaving Willy and I just on its fringes, more dimly lit and out of the way. We were seen to be important of course, as anyone accompanying her was, but nowhere near as important as her. That basically meant we had the best seats in the house, but without the pressure and fear of everyone watching us; because they weren't, they simply were not. Dinner was going to be fabulous, I could already tell.

We were collected directly from the red carpet and wound our way up narrow cobblestoned backstreets just as the sun was going down. It was a level of magic only relatable to one's wildest dreams. With my head hung out the window catching the last views of the sparkling sea shrinking away in the distance, I suddenly felt overwhelmed by an entirely new flavor of emotion. My mind started spinning in rewind, like one of those movie montages where they go backwards, rapidly scanning through a period of time in a character's life. It felt like I was watching on an invisible screen inside my soul, and with every frame that passed the one before, I realized with greater certainty that it was *my* life that I was seeing. I guess it wasn't until that car ride in France that I got a clear glance at the last eight months of my journey.

I'd been going so fast lately, focused on just keeping up, that I hadn't fully acknowledged the reality of what had actually been *happening*. But I saw it all that evening in the car. It hit me like a freight train just how incredible it all was. I had these friends now who made me feel accepted, validated and part of a team. We made this thing together and people liked it! People from all over the world were taking notice of something that I was part of, something that I loved! I couldn't quite tell if the feeling was fear or euphoria but it felt warm, heavy, and so powerfully overwhelming it made me cry.

So imagine the main drag of Cannes, a long spacious road flourished with boutiques, hotels and restaurants running parallel to the infinite deep blue. Then picture a mountain type thing behind it, laced with a narrow winding road allowing access to smaller, quieter places of business and residence. We arrived somewhere towards the top of this mountain, overlooking the entire landscape. Elizabeth dazzled the paparazzi and Willy and I stood happily in the corner while the homies got their shots. The restaurant was a tiny, utterly enchanting multi-level, exposed brick hole-in-the-wall establishment of your dreams. Tables were limited, entirely candle-lit and littered with a plethora of wondrous wild fresh flowers, like the movies.

Prepared for my usual scan the menu for low carb dishes I can order as is, I came to the conclusion that this was not the place nor the time to start asking for diabetic-friendly alternatives. Not with E Hurley, not in this exquisite establishment and not via a waiter who doesn't speak much English. No. Just flat out no. Rather go high and deal with it later.

After completing pleasantries with the restaurant owners, Elizabeth came over to where I sat, put her arms around my shoulders and whispered "I think you're going to enjoy this place, *baby Alex*, I picked it especially for you." Just as I turned around to ask her what she meant, an enormous wicker basket filled with the most utterly gorgeous fresh vegetables I have ever seen in my life was placed in the center of our table along with antipasto boards piled with prosciutto, salami, quail eggs and every variety of the creamiest French cheeses you could imagine. I could eat all of this stuff!!! I didn't even have to look at a menu! I was speechless. I didn't know what to say, it was all too much. I turned around in my chair, threw my arms around Elizabeth and wept quietly on her shoulder. I then ran around to give Willy a hug too, (because why the heck not?) and then the three of us drank wine and made short work of what was one of the dreamiest, delicious (problem free) dining experiences of my 25 years.

22

KEEP IT TOGETHER, MATE

Back in London Town and ready for season two, I felt less like a clueless foreigner and more like an in the know *semi*-local. I'd made sure to secure accommodation in the neighbourhood I wished I'd known about last time, the ultra hip and trendy Shoreditch, kind of like the Brooklyn of London. There's a constant electric buzz happening around the clock with the best coffee, markets, and bars all accessible by foot. The walls were graffitied with life-affirming quotes and it only took nine minutes to get to the studios. All in all, Shoreditch made a lot more sense.

I booked a quirky - what really should have been listed as a studio, one bedroom apartment on AirBnb. It was just up to the right of the main intersection on Shoreditch High Street. I followed the AirBnB instructions saved to my phone and was able to locate the big blue door directly behind a bus stop, under the overground train line, wedged between a hostel/laundromat to the left and a pizza joint to the right. After politely shimmying my way through the crowd of hipsters awaiting their bus to work,

I attempted the flippant lock box about six times before resorting to a good old fashioned karate kick which, believe it or not, actually worked! From here I rolled up my sleeves and lugged my four suitcases up to the top floor. The penthouse apartment was how he, the AirBnb man, described it. The gentleman's apartment in which I was renting referred to himself as "Mr." and, let me tell you, the mysterious Mr. had done a stately job with his 45 square meter penthouse. He'd cleverly added a sliding door in order to separate the bed from the kitchen and lounge area, the bathroom was essentially a functioning jigsaw puzzle in a cupboard, but the bricks were exposed and he left a chocolate bar and some daisies for me on the counter. So to sum up: I was far too impressed to be disappointed.

While lying in a sweaty heap on my new couch I almost forgot about the main reason I booked this spot (other than it being the only one I could afford in Shoreditch). Mr.'s penthouse also included an alleged private rooftop. So I made my way back into the stairwell and climbed the remaining few steps to what I had to assume would be the enticing private rooftop. Do you know what? It *was actually* fucking enticing, pigeons and train smog aside. I had a clear (ish) view of the neighborhood, spotted a couple of old foldable chairs in a box, that I could put together at a later date, and about the same, if not more space than the penthouse apartment itself! It was tremendous, quite frankly. I thought about how useful it would be for running lines, smoking in the nude, stretching, reflection and general outdoor activities.

Another key difference between this time in London and the last time was that I actually had things to do, events to attend. In fact, I had plans that night. Elizabeth had invited me to her 50th birthday party! With a few hours to unpack and to get myself looking presentable, Tom arrived on the train from Notting Hill with a lovely welcome hamper. We ate and drank while sitting on the floor as I dug through my suitcases for something to wear.

I wasn't feeling great due to some gnarly jetlag and a stubborn case of premenstrual high blood sugar. The latest problematic development I'd been dealing with since going off birth control a few months prior. I made the decision to go off birth control, oddly enough, because I'd been losing sleep over the idiotic fact that I was still smoking cigarettes. Obviously I was aware that smoking was bad for me, but I had also read somewhere that having diabetes and smoking was even more dangerous if you were on birth control. I knew I had to kick my filthy habit as soon as possible, but foolishly decided that eliminating birth control *instead* would allow me to continue smoking a little longer without feeling quite so bad about it. The motivated reasoning of an addicted mind, to be sure.

I'd been on birth control since I was 16 and never had any of the pimples, cramps, mood swings or the need for a larger sized jean. I'd always wondered what it must have been like to struggle with PMS, after hearing so many of my friends talk about the hell they went through every four weeks. By the time I arrived in London, I no longer needed to wonder. I was living it. Not only was I suddenly experiencing painful acne, brain fog, extreme fatigue and crippling anxiety, but my blood sugar was going bonkers again. It started when my estrogen dropped before my period or about a week before my period, and from there it was as though the insulin didn't work properly until the cycle finished.

It didn't matter how much I took or what I ate. I'd given myself almost three times the amount of insulin I'd normally take and my blood sugar just wouldn't come down. The premenstrual high blood sugar nightmare went on for two solid weeks every month. I didn't go back on the pill because I had already commenced the withdrawals and I was going to have to go off it at some stage anyway. Also, as specified before, I wanted to keep smoking.

Anyway, where was I? Oh yes. So I was feeling slightly tipsy and increasingly woozy and had fallen asleep on the floor. Tom had left at some point, but promised to call and wake me up when it was time to get ready for the party. I woke to the vibrations of my phone. "Alright, babe, you've got an hour until you have to leave" he said, like the good man that he is. "OK but what do I wear Tom?" I asked. "Anything but sneakers and jeans, babe. Go with your gut - you got this" was his reply.

In a panic, I threw on some leather pants from last season's wardrobe, my go-to Jimmy Choo Eleanor-hand-me-down boots, a fluorescent orange-lace midriff top that I'd received as a birthday gift from Elizabeth and a floor-length Alexander McQueen white trench coat (also involuntarily donated from the studio). I figured I'd just throw on the most impressive pieces I had with me and if all else failed, hopefully my wearing Elizabeth's thoughtful gift would make up for my underpreparedness.

With little to no clue what to expect, we (Harry, the driver, and I) drove a little under an hour away to the residential home of one of EH's friends. Feeling grateful for having had a nap, I was delighted by the arrival of a second wind, which kicked in just as we turned onto the driveway. The longest driveway I have ever been on, I might add, and one so aesthetically pleasing that, quite frankly, I didn't want it to end. Amber sun-drenched fields of wispy thigh-high grass with feathery bits on top danced in a gentle breeze, as families of deer lay in groups under broad-trunked weeping willows.

Before I got out of the car in front of this fairytale-like residence, I checked in with Glen who gave me a disappointing, yet recently predictable reading of 11 mmol/L (200 mg/dl). Assuming we would be eating and feeling quite hungry, I decided to save myself the embar-rassment of pulling out my needles in front of Elizabeth and her guests and gave myself 4 units. That sounds like a lot, but since my period was coming it was probably close to the right amount. I hoped the insulin would be a pal for once and get to work bringing my blood sugar down in time for preprandial canapés,which normally I would avoid like the plague, but this evening I was simply not willing to miss out on.

Elizabeth approached in a breathtaking corseted bone chiffon floor-length gown just as a gentleman ap-peared to remove my coat for me, revealing what I was starting to think was a slightly under-thought and some would say inappropriate ensemble. I thought for a mo-ment that I should grab my coat back to cover my fruity outfit, but got nervous and instead desperately hoped that my personality would make up for my lack of fash-ion sense.

I followed Elizabeth into the party, where an utterly bewitching gathering of pristinely dressed folks draped themselves over antique armchairs while sipping from crystal glassware that sparkled in what was left of the ro-mantic afternoon sun. Elton John (genuflect, genuflect!) stood in a corner and wore very small pink glasses. Dame

Joan Collins, (who I haven't mentioned yet, but played the part of the Queen Mother [and my grandmother] on *The Royals*) was there, too. She was explaining the ins and outs of her intricately embellished feather hat to a handful of other important-looking guests. I anxiously compiled a mental list of conversation topics if the opportunity presented itself. After a few moments wracking my brain for something witty, I conceded that I had nothing and that I was going to need a drink. To my delight, Elizabeth had organized vodka sodas to be made especially for me. She'd correctly assumed I wouldn't be partaking in the much more exciting fruity garnished cocktails that were on offer. "This is the lady who will be drinking the vodka sodas: keep them coming." she said and he listened. Oh boy, did he listen. My glass seemed to get magically refilled every time I looked away for a moment. A very sneaky bartender he was.

The party had started to move and guests were mingling around the house. I'd found myself in the most picturesque, candle-lit, glass greenhouse straight out of the Great Gatsby. I enjoyed a handful of cigarettes while slurring my way through an explanation about the best methods to keep fiddle-leaf fig trees alive. Elizabeth then floated by and saved me from a conversation with an audience that likely had their own staff to tend to their houseplants and announced that dinner was about to be served in the dining room. This I was more than thrilled to hear, as there was still next to nothing accompanying the alarming amounts of vodka swimming around in my stomach.

After locating my seat opposite Elizabeth, with grandma Joan to my right, I wondered who might be allocated the vacant seat to my left. The first course arrived and it involved raw fish, which unfortunately is a further restriction to my already extensive list of dietary requirements, unrelated to diabetes this time.

Unfortunately, I am quite severely allergic to raw fish. Who wouldn't want me over for dinner right? I'm quite possibly a waiter's worst nightmare (but what *can you eat?*). Thankfully, I wasn't the only one who was significantly sauced by this point, so nobody noticed that I didn't touch my entree. I quietly devoured some bread and butter and instantly remembered how long it had been since I'd tasted bread. Then I also remembered I had diabetes and that it had been a hot minute or two since I last checked in with Glen. The dining experience was fairly informal, so it was quite OK for me to nick off for a moment to check my blood sugar.

En route to the loo, I paused to appreciate an alluring figurative art piece. A mounted, life-sized glass coffin occupied by a nude lady mannequin with blood red lips, long dark hair and just a handful of daisies masking her nether-regions. Interesting, on to the ladies room. I felt momentarily refreshed after I splashed a bit of water on my face. I sat on the loo in the rose-scented bathroom and sent off a few texts to Mum, filling her in on my whereabouts, reading something like this: "Mummm! Elton John here. Oh and check out this weird naked dead lady. Wow, drunk 2 much tho. I'm fine. Crazy ass shit love yew smooch fun xxx."

Next I stood in front of the mirror and stared deeply inside my soul for a few minutes. I selected an essential oil misting spray from above the sink, spritzed myself with a cloud of lavender gypsy water and made my way back to the dining room.

It appeared that the vacant seat next to mine had been occupied during my trip to the loo by a man who was eating my abandoned entree and having a chat with Dame Joan. Eavesdropping a bit, I couldn't help but recognize the newcomer's velvety familiar voice. He turned to me as I not-so-gracefully sat down in my seat and said "Hello, my name is Hugh. Am I eating your entree?" Hugh Grant. I was sitting next to Hugh Grant. After seeing Elton John in his tiny pink spectacles, you might be surprised by how impressed I was. Notting Hill was one of my favorite movies of all time. I don't know if it was nerves or the alcohol taking the wheel for a moment, but I answered in a full-blown British accent.

"Hello Hugh!!! I'm Alex! I've just been to the loo, yes, you are, but please do, I'm allergic to fish."

"Tremendous, lovely to meet you Alex, I'm starving," he said.

"You're more than welcome Hugh. I'd hate for it to go waste. It's wonderful to meet you by the way, although I must say I feel like I've known you my whole life, you must get that all the time Hugh, forgive me, I'm waffling on. I've had quite a lot to drink," I said. This time in a muddled Australian accent with a British twang.

"What accent are you doing Alex?" said Hugh, understandably baffled.

"I am supposed to be doing an Australian accent, but I'm not sure what's happening Hugh." I was mortified.

"You should probably just stick to your Australian accent," he replied, helpfully. Off to a roaring start then.

Thankful for the interruption of the second course, a fragrant creamy risotto, I remembered I had failed to do the one thing I actually needed to do in the bathroom and therefore was left with no other choice but to whip Glen out here at the table. I managed an impressively inconspicuous finger-prick while nobody was watching. Sadly, my sugars were still super high, around 11 mmol/L (200 mg/dl), which baffled me. As drunk as I was, I definitely hadn't forgotten to take my four units of insulin. My need for food was greater than my need for balanced blood sugar at this point though, so I gave myself 4 more units and just a few bites of risotto to be safe. I could always just give the rest to Hugh considering we were already at the meal-sharing stage of our friendship.

Discreet injection delivery while sitting at a tightly-packed table was not something I had mastered yet. Unfortunately, Dame Joan Collins happened to gaze in my direction just as I did so and was alarmed by what she saw. "Is that a needle?! Oh God I can't stand blood, it makes me nauseous, I can't look at that." I quickly attempted to explain myself and apologized profusely, but Joan had now turned sharply in the other direction. At that moment I fantasized about being glued to the bottom of the ocean. Glumly, I gave myself the shot and frantically stashed all my medical instruments out of sight before anyone else outside of Hugh Grant noticed that I had just upset Dame Joan Collins.

Elizabeth, God bless her, intercepted this kerfuffle and invited me to join her for a cuddle and some shots (alcoholic, mind you, not insulin) over on her side of the table. Before partaking, I shoveled in a few mouthfuls of risotto against my disintegrating better judgement. I had some shots. I didn't need any shots, but everyone was having shots, so I had shots. I had to assume we were nearing the end of the celebration. It wouldn't be long until I was back in my penthouse shoe-box where I could give my deteriorating condition the attention it needed.

We sang to Elizabeth as she blew out the candles on her birthday cake. I ate a piece of cake without even bothering to check my blood sugars. It was delicious, we danced, we laughed and finally the night came to a roaring finish.

Absolutely shitfaced by this point, I hopped in the car and we made it all the way down the 10 minute-long driveway before I remembered I had left my expensive hand-me-down Alexander McQueen jacket in the cloakroom. We reversed all the way back up the drive, retrieved the McQueen, which naturally I threw up all over in a remarkably quick timeframe. I also needed to stop four or five times too on the way back to throw up on the sidewalk, and anything else that happened to be in my firing range. After this, I have a vague memory of being escorted up the stairs to my apartment by Harry.

Expressing my gratitude as coherently as possible, I locked the door behind me and attempted to remove my sticky leather pants (which, as you might imagine, was a nightmare in itself). I was successful with the pants, lied down, guzzled a Perrier and then of course remembered that I had *fucking* diabetes. I concluded in my flustered drunken state that diabetes was entirely (well, almost entirely) responsible for screwing with my evening. I knew how to drink. I'd learned at a very early age, as is the custom in Australia, and hadn't had an episode like tonight in a good five years. One of the most important things I'd learned during my adolescent drinking escapades is that drinking without eating is a mistake. A childish, irreversible mistake and one that pre-diabetes, was a hell of a lot easier to avoid.

Alright Glen, what's it gonna be? Give me your worst. I took a deep breath, closed my eyes and awaited my fate. Glen thrummed and whirred while he analyzed my blood. After taking a colossal amount of insulin, eight units over the course of about four hours, and having eaten just a couple of nibbles of bread, a few mouthfuls of risotto and half a piece of cake, I had absolutely no idea what to expect in terms of where my blood sugar sat. By some kind of miracle, Glen gave me a reading of 8 mmol/L (145 mg/dl), which was simply a gift from the heavens. I quickly evaluated that enough time had passed since my last dose and therefore it was unlikely I'd drop any further, allowing me to get some very much needed 'zeds' without the fear of, well, falling into a diabetic coma in my sleep! Yippee!!!

23

WILDLIFE

My decision to go off my birth control had far more consequences than I could have ever anticipated. I felt like I went backwards rather than forwards. Everything diabetes was up, down, and all over the place, and I wasn't coping well at all. After a couple of months I felt utterly defeated. I started to consider a bit of a backslide on this particular aspect of my path to optimum health and go back on birth control. As opposed to diving right in, I consulted extensively with my sister, Caley, who is a certified naturopath. She strongly advised me against it. She said that being on the pill completely shuts off our female hormones and that the synthetic replacements are no comparison. She told me that we need our female reproductive hormones for so much more than just reproduction.

They make us strong, they calm our nervous system, and allow us to feel happy. They give us healthy hair, skin and are vital for our libido. The pill also acts similarly to an antibiotic, mucking with our microbiome (our gut),which can lead to serious chronic gut issues. She also mentioned that 80% of our immune system is located in our guts. So, indirectly, the pill is messing with our immune systems and when you have an autoimmune disease like diabetes, this is probably not a good thing. To top it all off, the pill creates essential nutrient deficiencies that can lead to a host of other diseases later in life which, while living with type 1, we are already predisposed to. Then, of course, there are the fertility issues that many women face as they eventually come off of it.

Having all of this information, I felt like going back on the pill wasn't a great solution after all, but rather a questionable band aid. It would temporarily suppress a bunch of issues that I would eventually have to deal with anyway - issues I'd rather iron out now as opposed to right before I planned on having a baby. I knew it was possible for people with type 1 to give birth, but I also knew that it wouldn't be as easy as it would for women without type 1. Undoing the damage that seven years of birth control had done to my hormones wasn't something that was going to happen over night, but after weighing up my options, it was pretty clear I didn't have any other choice.

Up until now, diabetes had just been a game of numbers that I had learned to play. It was a math game. However, now that birth control wasn't artificially regulating my hormones, it became an unpredictable game of chance. A game of chance that didn't come with an instruction manual, or an option for a rain check. A game that I had to play while shooting the entire second season of The Royals. It was starting to feel like a game I couldn't win.

I'd be lying if I told you that season two of The Royals was a walk in the park, or season three, for that matter. The next couple of years filming both seasons were unlike any years I've had since being diagnosed. I was dealing with all the same challenges, but I wasn't actively trying to adapt or change my ways. I was simply getting from one day to the next. The fact that I came off birth control had exacerbated my issues and added another layer of horrifying unpredictability to my blood sugar adventures. I was so overwhelmed with all that was going on in my life, that I just sort of powered through like a robot and begrudgingly accepted the diabetic rollercoaster. I became very accustomed to daily spikes and drops. I had hypos most days which became a normal and expected occurrence. I'd try to quickly identify and treat them and then just get back on with it. It wasn't the most responsible plan, but the best I had at the time.

I had an overwhelming support system in my cast, crew, friends and family, and a hell of a lot more to be grateful for than I did to be sad about. When I look back on those crazy couple of years, even though I know it was a struggle, I don't remember it like that. I remember less about my struggle with my health and much more about all the other once in a lifetime incredible shit that happened.

I'll buzz you through the cliff notes.

During season two I walked in front of fifty galloping thoroughbreds without a scratch, got to burn down a large portion of the Red State Room that had been transformed into a makeshift carnival, filmed on a hundred foot yacht, smashed some horse riding scenes with E. Hurley and had a visit from Mum, my brother Joe, and my eighty-three-year-old absolute baller of a grandfather, who we call "EO." From here, I made a quick pit stop in NYC for another go at some press. I was much less anxious the second time.

Back in LA, I was slightly homeless. Luke and I had amicably gone our separate ways a while back, but remained friends. Tom flew over from London right as we learned we had been picked up for SEASON THREE - CAN YOU BLOODY BELIEVE IT! So we spent a couple months celebrating the above while living together like an old married couple in a bizarre, orient inspired Airbnb in Beverly Hills. Before heading back to his natural habitat (England), Tom helped me find a more permanent living situation. A cute little spot in *Holly-weird*, right off Sunset Blvd. It was very close to strip clubs and burger joints, which made me feel alive.

Willy and I then nipped down to Mexico City for the Latin American Upfronts. We cruised around with armed guards in bullet-proof cars and learned we were unexpectedly quite famous in Mexico, which was lovely and a bit nuts. From here I zipped back home to Sydney for some rejuvenation/booze in the sun with my remarkable clan.

Back in LA again, I shot an independent horror film about two sisters who get trapped underneath the fiberglass cover of a public swimming pool. I had mixed feelings about the experience and the finished product, but it was one that by no means I regret.

Regret nothing, guys. It's pointless.

For this next share, I'll expand on the cliff note as it's actually quite interesting and somewhat diabetes related. It's about marijuana also known as Mary Jane among other things. I'm sure you've all heard of it. My reasons were simple: It looked fun, I was curious and had researched the potential benefits of cannabis (in responsible doses) for insulin resistance. It remained a constant struggle for me since going off birth control. Now, understandably, you'll find a plethora of conflicting opinions and articles regarding medical marijuana, but I decided to take the leap and find out for myself. Here was a chance that cannabis could actually help bring my stubborn blood sugars down, and keep them there for longer than a minute or two at a time. A vast amount of my research claimed it would, so I was intrigued.

If I had to describe the inside of a Californian dispensary, I'd go with one of Willy Wonka's factories infused with an Apple store. The aesthetic is often bright, colorful, meticulously arranged, and the wild and fantastic varieties grown in far-flung locales are quite surreal to experience. Now, whether it's in an edible form: a gummy or a bar of chocolate, or the smoking variety: a pipe or a vape, I will tell you this much for free - cannabis in the United States is *fucking potent*. It wasn't at all like the puff or three I'd smoked of my friends' joints back home in Sydney. My advice is to really know what you're dealing with before lighting up or gobbling down, depending on your preference. This stuff can absolutely blow your head off if you're not careful. But, if you are careful, which I was, you'll find that in small doses, it does actually do wonders on the days where nothing else will bring your sugar down. Unsurprisingly though, there are a couple of drawbacks. The main one being that while using marijuana, you're *high*. It is great for winding down or days when you've got nothing going on, but isn't exactly the ticket in terms of everyday functionality. Also, cannabis has a remarkable ability to relieve pain and discomfort. It can basically eradicate shitty feelings and replace them with *very* relaxed, happy ones which is fantastic because, when the body and mind are relaxed, we reduce insulin resistance. Who doesn't like feeling relaxed and happy?

But seeing as symptoms of low blood sugar are included in the list of shitty feelings, they can often be masked by the effects of marijuana and therefore harder to identify. So, if you're not used to feeling high, this can be slightly confusing and alarming. Never underestimate the power of the green and be sure to check your blood sugar regularly. In my experience, nine times out of ten it will bring blood sugar down and, unless you're using a continuous glucose monitor, you likely won't be aware of it. I would say with a full degree of confidence that, personally, cannabis has had a beneficial, yet sometimes unpredictable effect. Anyway, that's my spiel on that. I recommend talking to a doctor or health professional to find out what is right specifically for you. Always use it with caution.

Before heading back to shoot the third season, Tom and I were invited on a free trip to Costa Rica where a few strange things happened. I covertly stole chocolates from Lance Bass suitcase in order to avoid a hypo on a bus ride during a relentless tropical thunderstorm. Tom had a very close encounter with a toothy Costa Rican sea snake. We extended the trip an extra week and nearly went home with a couple of stray dogs in tow.

This brought us to season three of *The Royals* where the madness continued. I ran around the London Zoo in the nude, painted head to toe in tiger stripes. Tom and I were taught basic dancing skills by Britney Spears' choreographer. We waltzed around the stages that had been transformed into a legitimate gingerbread man's house for a special "Musical Christmas" episode. I felt increasingly emotional with each majestic trip up to Blenheim Palace and basically just carried on piling up once in a lifetime memories into the little box inside my heart.

To sum up: seasons two, three and all that happened in between were a technicolored acid trip. A roller-coaster ride of blood sugar and euphoria. An invigorating, once in a lifetime near death experience of which I wouldn't have changed a single thing.

24

HARDENING UP

After completing the third season, I flew to a magical little town called Pagosa Springs, a quiet hidden gem in southwest Colorado. I was lucky enough to play a small part in a beautiful independent film called Shooting in Vain. I was there for about 10 days, but was only required on set for about five of them. During my time off, I drank tea in my rustic cabin and took solo expeditions around the rugged San Juan Mountains and the vast areas of national forest. Mostly, I just sat quietly, thought a lot, and reflected on the last couple of years. I let it all sink in. The stark change in pace and surroundings was like a gift from the heavens, and I could finally feel the ground beneath my feet.

It was during that week of fresh air and prolonged silence that I think I finally realized with full certainty that my system for managing my diabetes wasn't cutting it anymore. It allowed me to come to terms with my denial. I made peace with the fact that I'd spent the last couple of years running a race on a treadmill, on which I had decided for good or ill that my diabetes wouldn't be a priority. I was lucky I managed to come out of the last couple of years essentially unscathed, but I knew in my heart that I was living on the edge and cutting it close every time. I mean, heck, it kind of worked somehow for a while, but I knew I couldn't continue on like this for much longer. There had to be a better way for me to manage this thing. I wanted the ability to film anywhere, at any time, and have real versatility. This was just the beginning of my career and I refused to lower the bar for anything let alone fucking diabetes. I wanted the sky to be the limit. I wanted to have the option to film in the jungle swinging from a tree, or a desert war epic entirely on horseback, or to play a mad scientist trapped in an igloo in Antarctica. But I was tired now, and suddenly the frequent episodes of low blood sugar that I'd spent the last two years pushing under the rug were piled up right in front of me. I felt pretty disappointed in myself and a little bit scared. I knew I wasn't going to make it to Antarctica or the desert if I didn't get my condition under control.

After wrapping the film, it was back to LA where I dedicated a solid week to some much needed rest, recovery, and general life reflection. I only rose from the safety of my couch for bathroom and refreshment breaks. I was comforted by countless episodes of *Friends* and spent extensive periods gazing out the window, listening to birds and staring at trees. I came to the conclusion that it was time to put on my big girl pants in relation to a couple of things. Firstly, to give up the cancer sticks. It wasn't cute anymore. I was almost twenty-seven and becoming increasingly anxious and disappointed in myself with every puff. Secondly, to revisit the idea of a continuous glucose monitor.

So the TV went off, pants went on and I was ready to kick this shit into gear. First stop was a visit to the vape store, where I purchased a nerdy-looking device along with some blueberry infused nicotine oil. The vape man was very enthusiastic and congratulated me on taking this first step towards my desired ciggie-free lifestyle. Fuck yeah. Look at me go.

Next up on the self improvement train, I spent the rest of the day watching YouTube videos of people talking about continuous glucose monitors. I wanted to hear from people who actually used the things. I'd been so overwhelmed and traumatized by the idea initially (if you'll remember) I wrongly or rightly associated them with failure or a sign of weakness. I was also simply grossed out by the look of them and hated the idea of being attached to something. I didn't want to be reminded of my condition every time I looked at it and I didn't want anyone else to see it. After trying it for all of 24 hours some years ago, I convinced myself that I didn't like the way it felt, that it was physically limiting, poorly constructed, inaccurate, and essentially pointless. But I was very angry back then and I've had a few years to get over myself. My priorities have shifted and I've grown up a lot. The only thing I was concerned about at this point was finding a system better than the one currently in place.

I came across a video that was made by a good-looking shirtless guy named Dave. He was standing by a pool. Dave had his continuous glucose monitor attached to his impressively ripped abdomen and appeared to be without a care in the world. He even said that his only regret was that he didn't find it soon enough. His device did seem to look a lot smaller than the one I tried on all those years ago.

Dave is a personal trainer from Sydney. He sees up to six clients back-to-back on a typical day. These clients require his full attention, and, as we know, it's very hard for someone with type 1 who's worrying about their levels to give anyone their complete and undivided attention.

> *"I was having to excuse myself in the middle of a session to check my blood sugar, which was distracting and I was sick of putting my client second to my diabetes. Now, if anything goes wrong, I get an alert on my Dexcom (the company that makes the devices). It's great because I'm not shifting focus all the time, constantly worrying about my blood sugar. My Dexcom offers a peace of mind that allows me to give my full attention to my wonderful clients."* - Dave, personal trainer

Well, *shit*, Dave didn't mention anything about feeling physically limited. There was no mention of discomfort, nothing negative at all really and, to be frank, Dave looked pretty hot doing it.

Dave went for it. He slapped that bad boy on and he's never looked back. Dave's not sitting in an office chair all day either, he's lunging and planking and Russian twisting that shit. Alright! Yeah Dave! Way to help me put things in perspective. Legend.

Next, I found the YouTube channel of a lovely lady named Emily. As far as I could gather, Emily was an all-business high-end stylist from London also living with type 1. She was all-smiles with a radiant glow about her as if she had just been on a stimulating jog. However, it turns out she had just got home from hitting five different department stores and was preparing for an afternoon of back-to-back client fittings. How impressive. She mentioned how difficult it was to adapt to her diagnosis, that "I was starting to think I no longer had what it took. I hated that I didn't have the energy to give my clients 150%. I didn't have time to prioritize my blood sugar and was out of steam before the day even began." She was also a big fan of the continuous glucose monitor, saying, "The CGM has allowed me to continue doing the thing I love most and to the best of my ability. It breaks my heart to think I almost considered switching careers. I wear the sensor on my hip, where nobody can see it, allowing me to maintain my image which I pride myself on it's an important part of my job."

I didn't know you could wear it on your hip? That was a lot more appealing than having it in the middle of my stomach Ridley Scott/Prometheus-style. I desperately didn't want to give up the option of wearing a midriff. Midriffs are kind of my jam. Emily went on to talk about something else I was not aware of: the fact that her mother, who lives 400 miles away, is connected to her CGM. Oh God, I wondered how excited this would make Pippy G. Emily mentioned that this was a great feature because, in the case of an emergency, when you're sleeping or can't get the alerts, you have the peace of mind that someone will be watching and can send help remotely.

Clearly the technology came a long way in the last few years. The idea of additional support from Mum while I was alone in various corners of the earth sounded pretty great. Emily wrapped it up by clarifying that "Before CGM, I was just surviving. With CGM, I am living my absolute best life." I wished I was friends with both Dave and Emily. I was a bit in awe of these brave and capable legends, making me feel a bit silly for worrying about this whole thing. I decided to focus on figuring out how quickly I could join the CGM club.

According to Google, *Dexcom* was making the best CGMs on the market. *Dave* and *Em* both went with Dexcom, so I called them straight off the bat. All ordered and on the way, I felt giddy with excitement and curiosity. I spent the next few days sitting by the front door vaping and watching the door for a delivery. During a quick shower-break I was startled by the ring-a-ding-ding I'd been waiting for. In quick succession, I leapt out of the shower, wrapped myself in a towel, and slid my wet feet across the hardwood floor to the front door like a figure-skater. This ensured I would catch Ronnie the postman, before he assumed I wasn't home and left. Not waiting another day, Ronnie! I apologized to Ronnie for my lack of clothing and for dripping shampoo all over his signing sheet. I wished him well, closed the door behind me, and ripped the UPS bag open while standing in the nude.

While opening the starter kit box, I remembered that I knew nothing about how this thing worked or where to even begin. I would need to read the instructions, which I've always hated doing, so I rapidly rinsed the shampoo out of my hair, threw on the nearest pants and begrudgingly got started with the extensive users guide.

After ruining two perfectly good sensors, thanks to my impatience with printed instructions, I thankfully still had four sensors remaining in the box. For the second time only, since being diagnosed, I turned to the online diabetes community for advice.

"Diabetic Daniella" would be my next online guide. Daniella was a very cheerful 13-year-old YouTuber. Her helpful videos guided me step by step through the application process with an uplifting, American, cheery can-do attitude, which made it a bit fun even. She started by introducing herself as Diabetic Daniella while holding the box up to the screen, smiling from ear to ear, saying "Isn't it *beautiful*? I *love* it. OK so let's get started..." How heartwarming. Thanks to Daniella, the munchkin, who clearly knew how to follow instructions, I was locked-and-loaded and ready to go. I couldn't help but wonder if my failed assembly of a recently-purchased Kallax bookcase was *not* in fact IKEA's fault at all.

Surprised by how stoked I was feeling with this thing on, I thought I might even take it for a spin. I quickly changed into some workout clothes and took a few 'Dexcom selfies,' which I shared with a handful of people before heading to Griffith Park for a hike with my new companion, the Dex.

It was a cool day, but I decided to leave my sweater in the car in the hope that fellow hikers might notice the intriguing futuristic medical device attached to the back of my arm. Maybe I'd get to chat about my nifty new robot friend and show random people all the neat things I'd learned. I'd gone from 0 to 100 in a matter of three days on the Dexcom thing. I was bordering on being completely stoked by this point. All of a sudden I felt like I was part of an exclusive and mysterious club, one that represented perseverance and strength as opposed to weakness or disability. I felt confident, hopeful, with a newborn sense of control.

To my disappointment, even though I was specifically angling my Dexcom out for optimal viewing, nobody seemed to notice. However, on the final incline before reaching the top of the mountain, I heard an un-familiar beep coming from the Dexcom. "FALL RATE ALERT" was the notification that accompanied the jingle. The notifications all came straight to my iPhone, which was super nifty. I was at a level of 5.2 mmol/L (95 mg/dl) and two arrows to indicate that it was going down quickly. It was working! I mean, I knew it prob-ably would, based on what Dave and Em had said in their videos, but this confirmed it. It made sense; I had eaten a salad about an hour ago and my bloods were in good shape after eating, but this hike was intense cardio, which understandably had created a further blood sugar dip that likely wouldn't have happened had I not just climbed a mountain. I wasn't feeling shaky or disori-ented as the Dex was ahead of the game. It let me know we were going low, but it gave me enough warning time to avoid it. Feeling like I'd just uncovered the secret to living with type 1 diabetes, I chewed on a couple of glucose tablets, followed by a nut bar and pounded the rest of the path with vigor. I checked the Dex once more before heading back down and the second arrow had disappeared, leaving just the one arrow no longer pointing down, but horizontal again, which indicated that my sugar was stable and I was no longer at risk of having a hypo.

I was absolutely mesmerized by the intelligence of this device. There was a tiny little hair-sized sensor beneath my skin that calculates how much glucose is in my blood every 5 minutes, noting each reading with a dot, that eventually forms a line showing me the fluc-tuation of my blood sugar over a 24 hour period. I am able to tell it when I want to be notified, based on my goals. So if my bloods dip below 4 mmol/L (70 mg/dl) , the Dex is programmed to let me know and the dot will drop out of the predetermined safe range, which is the grey middle section of the graph, and fall into the red section of the graph. If my blood sugar rises above 9.7 mmol/L (174 mg/dl), the dot moves up into the yellow section and notifies me that I am high.

By no means did this initiate an early retirement for Glen. The Dexcom had a lot to offer, but technology is technology at the end of the day and it was prone to occasional inaccuracies or signal losses. Glen was my first, day-one, true homie in the battle against diabetes and would remain on call and close by if ever the Dexcom was having an occasional meltdown/malfunction. All that said, boy was I looking forward to giving my butchered fingertips a bit of time off from Glen's needle.

I've been rolling with the Dex for four years now (at the time of writing this memoir) and not once since strapping it on have I had to ice heavily perforated finger pads or choose which of my pointers are ravaged less and therefore most fit for a puncture. Hallelujah!

25

CAN I HAVE YOUR ICE CREAM, PLEASE?

While preparing to go back to London for season four of *The Royals*, I was feeling *invincible*. With no distractions whatsoever, I dedicated most of my time to chasing the straight line on my Dex. Now that I had this intelligent machine, I felt there was an even better chance of achieving next to non-diabetic blood sugar. It gave me the confidence to correct without hesitation, to tighten my numbers, to interfere without thinking twice. I trusted that the Dex would let me know if I'd taken it too far and would catch me if I was to fall. It was a full time job and really all I thought about, but I figured by the time I got back to work it would all feel like second nature.

I'd given our costume designer, Charlie Jones, a heads-up prior to my arrival. I'd sent her pictures of the Dexcom and explained that the sensor could be moved every 10 days to either my stomach, hip, or the back of my arm to help her plan for particularly tricky or revealing costumes. Charlie was a boss, an absolute pro and an enormous support during the previous three seasons. She assured me she would be able to work around my new friend Dex. Her only concern was Eleanor's frequent intimate scenes, but she was on the case and would speak to the director prior to any upcoming nudey scenes. The camera crew came prepared with some clever strategies to work around the mini-computer stuck to my ass without having to interfere with the visionary imagery or sexual impact of the scene, which are obviously essential components of our show! An example of this strategic and successful planning was during an important scene where Eleanor visited her boyfriend Jasper in the hospital. He had recently and horrifically been shot in the chest while defending the Royal Family.

Eleanor wanted to physically show her appreciation and did so by orchestrating an in-house striptease. I was dressed in a stunning La Perla Ambra diamond-embellished bodysuit complete with a floral lace garter, sheer thigh highs and arduously assembled by the costume team. To ensure the shots had only skin and zero robot, the director made sure the cameras were set on the bits of my body that were Dexless with a slow-motion pan. No need for last minute camera adjustments, no need for last minute costume changes. The crew was like family. They were caring, supportive and meticulous when it came to working around my new device. Business. As. usual. Well, mostly.

In terms of *blood sugar control*, the pursuit of the straight line became progressively harder to maintain once my schedule beefed up. Sporadic meal times, irregular sleeping hours and forever-changing call times meant I was just busy, really *effing busy*, which obviously allowed less time for my other full-time job of never letting the dots on the Dexcom graph move out of the grey.

Old habits don't die easy though, at least they didn't for me. Whatever sliver of hesitation I might have considered before giving myself correctional insulin had vanished completely now I had the Dex. I didn't think twice about pulling out the pen and jabbing myself in the leg en route to set whenever I was presented with a number outside of what I believed was within acceptable range. Alerts started chiming throughout takes, reminding me of insulin I had forgotten I'd even taken. Overall, I was having less hypos, as, most of the time, I was able to spring into action when needed. But the hypos I *didn't* catch in time, the ones that happened after a day of recklessly stacking insulin,[8] were increasingly severe and often without warning. The Dex couldn't keep up with the vast amounts of insulin in my system that eventually started to work all at once.

So, as the story went, Eleanor was pursuing a career in interior design, specifically in hotels. She was making her way across the world visiting establishments in need of a makeover and leaving them new and improved, refreshed and jazzy "Hoteleanors." The bulk of the story-line was brought to life by the art department, who did an astounding job of exactly replicating the interiors of various internationally-renowned hotels. But, in order to really bring this puppy to life, production

---

8   *Insulin stacking is described as an insulin correction within three hours of a previous correction. Insulin stacking is often equated with 'emotional bolusing,' which is an emotional reaction to high blood glucose levels in the form of insulin overcorrection. I recommend further reading on these concepts, as they're universally recognized as a common psychological struggle for people living with type 1 diabetes.*

gave us the go-ahead to capture the essence of one of these exotic hot spots on location. The powers that be decided on the Amalfi Coast as it's a reasonably quick trip from London and, as I learned very quickly, is one of the most breathtaking corners of the earth. AKA a cinematic slam-dunk.

We weren't *Game of Thrones* though, were we? It was just myself along with a handful of our crew who came over from London along with a few local Italians we'd recruited to help us out during the three day adventure. There was no prepaid, organized arrangement whereby we were given permission to shut down public spaces in order to get the shots we needed. We just kinda pinged about from cliff edges to narrow cobblestone alleyways, ducked into nearby hotel rooms for makeup and cos-tume changes, rehearsed amongst the crowds and only when we were absolutely ready to grab a shot would we discreetly and politely ask the tourists and locals to shimmy out of the frame.

We managed to steal a super-sexy drone shot of Eleanor gazing longingly at a couple canoodling on the jetty. Our success continued with a stalker sequence, where I was to duck beneath some clotheslines and weave my way out of a predator's eyesight, into a dimly-lit back alley. The reading of Jasper's letters while overlooking the Meditteranean Sea scene was a walk in the park as it was shot in the back of the hotel where we were staying.

Eventually, all that was left on the shot list was a rather ambitious sequence that would take place on the wide, steep steps of the medieval Amalfi Cathedral. They wanted a shot of Eleanor either walking down or sitting on the steps, reflecting wistfully and preferably alone. Or as close to it as possible. Clearing tourists out of a 24-hour hot-spot like this was going to be border-line impossible, but the show must go on and the direc-tor insisted this shot was essential. While we waited for the crew to work it all out, Tina (makeup), Charlie (cos-tumes), and I sat in a cafe at the bottom of the iconic cathedral stairs and contemplated lunch as we waited for instructions.

Before we put our order in, I checked in with Dex. So far today Dex had been giving me hellishly high readings. I had woken up high (in the yellow of the graph), so I had a tiny breakfast (a poached egg), with double the insulin I normally would have taken. I had turned off the high alerts as every time I heard the *PING*! it made my skin crawl. I was hoping that after walking around for the last few hours, they might have come down, but they hadn't, which made me *really re-ally* angry. Assuming that I must be due for my period, I pulled out my insulin and gave myself another five units. That was three more than I would normally take to cover the charcuterie board, iced coffee and salad we just ordered. I assumed the scene was going to involve my running up and down the Amalfi cathedral steps. So I was hopeful that a big dose along with a bunch of exercise would do the trick and straighten my line. I had started to become truly obsessed with that beautiful straight line. The coffees arrived in time for me to take a big sip, just as I was called for rehearsal. This was fine by me since a little cardio to help kick the insulin into gear would hopefully bring my number down in time for when the food arrived.

Up and down the sixty-five stairs I went, first from the right, then the left, then stopping halfway and wait-ing in position for the camera. This rehearsal, albeit simple, was taking longer than I anticipated. As I sat there peeking through sun-squinted eyes, I noticed the waiter had returned with part of our order. I felt a tad stressed about not having the Dex with me for this longer-than-anticipated rehearsal and being unable to communicate from my high-altitude, isolated position. I took comfort in the fact that even though I'd taken insulin prior to my ascension, the likeliness of it working already was slim, and that realistically it would only take me a few minutes to get within reach of whatever Tony the waiter had just laid down on the table.

"Alright Alex, come down, we need to adjust something before we can shoot. you've got ten minutes or so." boomed one of the AD's.

Fabulous, that leaves me with a solid seven minutes for refueling - *plenty of time.* Back at the table, I scooped up a handful of tantalizing salami and several sheets of delicate cheese before the person who yelled at me last time had started up yelling at me again.

"Ricardo is going to act as a barrier, enabling a clear path, go back to the top, Al, we don't have long."

Ricardo was the policeman responsible for manning the cathedral steps who just so happened to be a fan of the show and agreed to help us out in exchange for a quick selfie for his wife.

Right! OK, so we're just waiting on me then?

"Coming!!!" I yell out.

Wiping my cheese fingers on my bare legs, I made my way back to the top, and remembered I had completely forgotten to check my Dex.

You know what comes next. A good ol' fashioned, drastically inconvenient hypoglycemic terror attack. Hello, darkness, my old friend. Today, our old friend hypo appeared resplendent. It was accompanied by the traditional symptoms of sweating and paranoia and alongside my strong will to not fuck up what was probably our only opportunity to get this *essential* shot. I went up and down the steps about three or four times before I started to feel light headed and disoriented. In an attempt to not freak myself out or jump to conclusions, I reminded myself that it was hot as balls today, and that what I'm feeling could easily just be slight heat exhaustion mixed with increasing hunger. But, I'd played this game of lying to myself many times before - I was desperate to be right just this one time. I stood in position at the top of the stairs. The crew looked blurry, then everything was blurry. I knew they'd called action and I could make out the cameras in position, but my legs were so shaky now that I feared going back down the stairs, as I might trip and stack it on the hard concrete. I didn't know what to do. I was fairly certain I was having a hypo by this stage and it was terrifying at this high altitude. I was sweating profusely and needed to sit down, to get out of the scorching sun and find some sugar. I retreated to the covered entry of the cathedral (at the top of the stairs) and noticed the security guard was eating an ice cream. Plucking up as much foggy courage as I could, I asked the gentleman, "Excuse me sir, could I please have your ice cream?" He looked at me strangely until I finished with the helpful directive phrase "I think I'm going to faint," which motivated him more. Lying out on the cool tiles, I inhaled the stranger's ice cream and tried to keep my eyes open while I waited for Charlie and Tina who I knew wouldn't be far away.

Right as I felt like I couldn't stay awake any longer, the girls arrived with glucose and Glen, who I needed, as the Dex I'd left on the table was out of range. 1.2

mmol/L (21 mg/dl) was the reading Glen gave me. Eventually and thankfully, I was able to gather myself as the glucose kicked in and the crowd of curious tourists dispersed from the circle they'd understandably formed around my limp, sweaty, humiliated body.

The Dex has helped me in many ways to have a more immediate understanding of what my blood sugar is doing on a daily basis. However, it can't stop insulin from working or slow it down if I've had too much, or save me from inevitable hypos that come from stacking insulin as a means to feed my obsession with control.

Dexcom or not, I gave myself insulin as though I knew everything about it, as though I was more powerful than it, but I was not. All I knew in that moment was that the way I was using insulin had nearly killed me a lot more times than being slightly "high" ever has. I was embarrassed, but I'd been embarrassed in situations like this many times before. What I hadn't felt yet was scared, not of diabetes, but of myself.

I was so excited by everything the Dexcom had to offer. The easily accessible, always available information, the freedom and the peace of mind. Although I suppose I was pretty naive in my assumption that it would solve all of my problems, be the answer to my prayers and somehow teach me how to do this thing. The issue remained the same; I felt like I was failing. All I wanted was a long life, to be healthy, like everybody else. I wanted to live as long as I would have prior to this disease or at least I wanted the best shot I could get, but every time I tried to interfere, I made it worse. For the remainder of the shoot, I tried really hard to think twice before giving myself correctional shots. The severity of the lows/hypo's, albeit less frequent, had scared the shit out of me. This was good in some ways, as it led to less lows, but overall it felt like I was being forced to give up the pursuit of that *straight line*, obliged to accept defeat and therefore imperfection. I *hated* that.

So, for the time being, my diabetes hat went back on the rack as I was sick of trying to make it fit. I instead focused on getting everything I could out of what was left of the season. As a result, I was better able to immerse myself completely in what was left of the shoot, though I feared this devil-may-care approach may come back to bite me. There was a lot of magic left on the schedule and I was OK with letting my diabetes just do what it was going to do for a while. It was always there though, like a faint ringing in my ear, or a vexing itch I couldn't scratch.

We'd been so incredibly fortunate as a cast and crew. It was rare for a TV show to continue for two seasons, let alone four. At the end of every season, I made peace with the possibility that this one could be the last. I was mostly OK with it because I was just so damn grateful that it had happened at all. For the last couple months of this incredible fourth season, my whole heart was there with the art, my great love and the magic.

We filmed "*The Royal Wedding*" episode in the medieval Ely Cathedral, which was about two hours out of Central London. I remember tracing my eyes over the ethereal aesthetics for the first time as an orchestra and a choir of over one hundred men and women rehearsed a version of "Creep" by Radiohead, which they performed for the episode. Creep is one of my all-time favorite songs; and Radiohead is my absolute favorite band. The acoustics, the lyrics, the vast beauty of it all was almost too much to take in. It was so overwhelmingly moving that it made my entire body tremble. Even after four years of living different versions of this dream of a job, I still couldn't quite believe it was really me who was standing there.

We shot at Blenheim Palace for what I knew could possibly have been the very last time. Blenheim Palace is the stately principal residence of the Dukes of Marlboro built in the eighteenth century in Oxfordshire, England. A UNESCO World Heritage Site and the birthplace of Winston Churchill, this immaculate monolith became a sort of second home for our production, as it provided us with all of the exterior shots for our scripted Royal Palace. On our last shooting day at Blenheim, I stood on the sandstone landing that overlooked a vast courtyard and sweeping countryside views, benevolently observing my forever-friends beside me as we beamed under a perfect blue sky. The smiling faces of one hundred or more supporting actors surrounded us, entirely still as together we listened to a bone-chilling rendition of "I Vow To Thee, My Country," played by a live marching band.

On the very last day of the season four shoot, I was filled with mixed emotions. I was proud and grateful, as much as I was sad and nostalgic. I wiped off my Eleanor makeup for the last time, possibly ever. I took a quick moment to breathe it all in one more time, before jumping in the car with Harry. Then, I closed my eyes and told myself over and over again that it wasn't all just a dream.

26

ZAK THE MAN

I was now back in LA and the fourth season of *The Royals* was in the can. After all the adrenaline had worn off, I was back to being just regular ol' AL. On one particularly flat day, I was interrupted from my wallowing state by call from my lawyer who informed me that his 19-year-old son had just been diagnosed with type 1 and was wondering if I would meet up with him. He thought it would be helpful to hear from someone going through the same thing, that perhaps I might be able to offer him some tips. Admittedly, my enthusiasm for diabetes related stuff at the time was like that of a limp balloon, wilted around the edges, still brightly colored but covered in dust, anticipating the spike of a safety pin and ready to be thrown in the trash.

If Zak was diagnosed a year ago, I likely would have said that everything was going to be fine and that it was his lucky day, as I had the answers to everything. A year ago I might have swanned down to the cafe, hair freshly blow-dried, wearing one of my classic black-on-black ensembles, brimming with confidence. But I'd had a rough trot lately and came to the harsh conclusion that my confidence was all a facade.

Regardless of what I felt I had to offer, of course, I wanted to be there for Zak. To shoot the *diabetic shit*. Plus, I'd never spoken to anyone with type 1 before; could be helpful for both of us. I was expecting to meet a frail, scared young fellow with the weight of the world on his shoulders, much like how I felt from time to time (even now).

I arrived flustered after battling the traffic on Sunset Blvd. and a particularly challenging parking situation. I dodged a very close collision with an exiting patron, which didn't really matter because I tripped and fell on my ass in front of everyone, thanks to a poorly tied shoelace. I recovered with considerable grace and asked the hostess if Zak had arrived yet. I was hoping he hadn't for obvious reasons, but of course he had.

Walking over to the table, I noticed that Zak looked the opposite of what I imagined a 19-year-old boy newly-diagnosed with type 1 diabetes would look like. He was a tall and handsome *man*, I would call him, not a *boy*. He was also dressed sharp as shit in a light blue button-down, cool jeans, cool shoes, cool as shit sunglasses resting on top of his stylish hair, and a smile on his face that made me feel like I'd known him for years. Zak rose from the table, walked around to introduce himself and, before returning to his seat, he pulled mine out for me. Like, I don't even remember the last time a male of any age pulled my chair out for me. I was absolutely flabbergasted by this young man's calm, collective, chill vibe as he sipped on a herbal tea confidently, leading the conversation, asking me about how the shoot went, how the jet lag was treating me, etc etc.

After I placed an order for a Burrata salad that Zak assured me would be delectable we pulled out our kits and injected in unplanned, yet complete synchronicity - he looked like he'd been doing it for years. I took the opportunity to mention the elephant in the room and asked Zak how he was dealing with all this (referring to our diabetic bits and pieces). He replied with a shrug of his shoulders, a chuckle and a smile, "Oh, you know, could be worse! I'm just glad I know what was making me feel so shit!" HA! He was entirely unfazed! I was simply enamoured with this guy! He just seemed to be taking it all in stride. He didn't stop smiling and did this little follow-up chuckle thing that warmed my heart every time he talked about something that clearly excited him, like how he was currently taking meetings for marketing positions at Facebook, YouTube and fucking google! or how in a few weeks he was leaving for Europe where he would spend the summer backpacking with his mates! It was so refreshing and encouraging to talk to this guy. He made me feel better about myself while putting the thought in my head that maybe I don't need to be so freaked out all the time and that perhaps I could take a leaf out of Zak's book and get better at going with the flow.

Naturally, Zak *insisted* on paying the check, which was absurd considering how little I felt I had helped him and how massively (he likely didn't know) he'd helped me. He asked me who my doctor was. "I don't really have one actually" I said. To which super-Zak replied, "I'll have my mom get you in touch with Dr. Peters. She's amazing. I think you'll really like her."

Before going our separate ways, I hugged Zak for a bit longer and tighter than he was probably expecting. I told him to not be a stranger and to call me if he ever wanted to chat. He thanked me and told me to do the same. I drove home feeling better about my diabetes than I had in months, inspired, renewed, possibly with a new doctor, but most of all, with a new friend.

Shortly after our lunch date, I received an email from Zak's Mum Lucy. She kindly offered to write a letter of introduction to Dr. Anne Peters to find out if there was any way she could squeeze me into her fully-booked schedule. As weird as this may sound, I was starting to feel like Zak's diagnosis, albeit a definite bummer for him, had been enormously helpful for me. All of a sudden, I had this incredible support from this amazing family! It felt like they had taken me under their united wing, as opposed to the original plan, which was supposed to be me taking Zak under mine. Funny how life works.

Anyway, by some kind of miracle, Dr. Peters offered me an appointment for three weeks away, which allowed me a convenient window of time for one more little adventure.

27

IT'S NOT ME, IT'S THE MONSTER

To bring you up to speed, at some stage during the later seasons of *The Royals* I developed a mad crush on one of the directors, James. James, or "Marty" as I decided to call him, very quickly became my favorite person on the planet. He's whip smart, grounded, endlessly fascinating, gentle, mysterious, and an intimidatingly gifted creative. We started hanging out pretty much all the time. I think he was a bit scared of me at first, but fear and intrigue are solidifying elements of love we found.

Anyway, we were fresh to death at that stage, the world was our oyster, etc. James had invited me to join him on a quick work trip to Paris, which naturally I accepted in a heartbeat. I'd asked James to interfere if ever he caught me shooting up on the fly, as my old habits had resurfaced since finishing the *The Royals* shoot, and I was finding it hard to trust myself again. I didn't have any problems when we were together cruising around Paris. Knowing he was there and kept an eye on me forced me to re-think my decisions and ask myself before he did if I really needed the shot I was about to give myself. So, basically I was a child who did the right thing when being watched by an adult. Then, as soon as I was left to my own devices, the faint ringing in my ear grew to an amplified high-pitched screech. The control monster, the monster that caused me to take too much insulin and get myself into trouble, took a hold of me. I had a horrendous hypo while I was by myself on the streets of Paris. My phone had run out of battery, I had run out of glucose, and it was raining. I was lost and ended up on the floor of a cafe pouring sugar packets into my mouth, soaking wet, shaking like a junkie.

It occurred to me on the flight back to Los Angeles that there was not a single destination I had been over the past five years that hadn't included a near death experience brought on by self-inflicted hypoglycemia. Regardless of how good I was at convincing myself that these hypos were an acceptable result of my pursuit for perfect blood sugar, I finally started to realize that all the evidence pointed toward me being in over my head. To break this dangerous pattern something would have to change. I was ready to put my ego aside, to accept defeat, and to ask for help. There had to be a better way.

Contrary to every previous doctor appointment, I arrived at Dr. Peters' office entirely numb. Timid, if you can even believe it. Long gone was the Alex who walked in looking for a fight and dismissing whatever advice the doctor might have had for me before I'd even sat down in the chair. I didn't want to fuck this up. I was ready for some guidance and feeling nervous. I sat in the waiting room and attempted to steady my pen-holding hand. I got halfway through filling out my forms when a beautiful woman dressed in scrubs squatted in front of my clipboard, put a hand on my knee, and introduced herself. "Hey girl, my name is Rachel. I work for Dr. P.

How you doing this morning?" I don't know what it was about Rachel, but as soon as my eyes locked into hers I felt like, without having to say anything at all, she knew me and she knew exactly how I was feeling. "I'm OK, I guess, thank you for asking," I replied with my best effort not to cry. "Why don't you come with me, babe. Let's get you weighed. Dr. P is the best. We're going to take care of you, OK?" Rachel took my hand and whizzed me through the pre-consultation stages, which felt more like a buddy system than a doctor-patient procedure. She stood next to me while I got on the scales, waited outside the loo while I peed in the cup, and after taking some blood for an A1C test (blood sugar), she sat next to me and asked about Australia while we waited for Dr. P.

Rachel made me feel so welcome. This was the least doctor-y doctor's office I had ever been to. The energy there was light, staff members whistled about the place, and popped their heads in to say hello. I felt like I was being hugged by a bunch of people I'd never met before, and it was slightly overwhelming. Rachel peaced out, likely to go make someone else feel as welcome as she made me. She closed the door behind her and told me Dr. Peters would be in shortly.

I was so eager to meet Anne that I'd torn all my bloody fingernails off in the three minutes since Rachel left. Maybe it was because she came with a soaring recommendation from the only person I knew living with the same condition as me. Or maybe it was because I had finally surrendered. I think it was mostly that.

I could see shadows of feet approaching the gap under the door, then I heard the shuffling of the clipboard being removed from the slot. As soon as she entered the room my nervousness evaporated. Dr. Peters was tall, slender and had shoulder-length dark hair. She was smiling through her eyes as well as her mouth and she radiated maternal energy as she approached me feeling so small in my chair. Before she had the chance to introduce herself, I burst into tears again. Correction: I *wailed*. There was no stopping it, I couldn't keep it down. It was as though everything I'd been holding inside for the last five years had just reached maximum internal capacity and was finally released. I didn't even know this woman! I had no idea if she would be able to get through to me, but I wanted her to try so desperately. It all just hit me at once.

"I can tell you're a special one," she said as she passed me a tissue. "It's going to be OK, I can promise you that." After taking a few deep breaths to steady my quivering vocal chords, I gave her the spiel. I told her I'd been traveling on a literal rollercoaster since the day I was diagnosed. I'd done everything in my power to manage this thing, but that I felt I was failing. I told her I'd diligently do anything she said and I was ready to follow someone else's guidelines. I said that I thought I kept going low because I was so scared of what would happen to me if I left my sugar high. I told her that I felt stuck and that, no matter how hard I tried, I was pretty much chasing an unpredictable yoyo.

It all just came out. Nothing was held back. I asked her frantically if she thought my frequent hypos had done any permanent damage to my brain. I asked her if I was going to lose my eyesight from how regularly my blood sugar was high. I told her all I wanted to do was be an actor, but was terrified I would end up dead after one of the lows I kept having as a result of my desperate attempt to avoid the equally shitty alternative of developing long-term complications from high blood sugar.

When I was done telling my sob story, I wiped my drenched face with my sleeve and looked up at Anne who was flipping through my Dexcom report. She'd printed off graphs from the last 90 days and was mathematically calculating the results with a focused and slightly stunned look on her face.

"Alex, I have the numbers in front of me. You have an A1C (average blood sugar reading) of 4.5 mmol/L (81 mg/dl), which is a little bit lower than I'm comfortable with, and explains the lows you speak of, but you need to trust me when I tell you that your control is outstanding. You're actually in the top 2% of type 1 patients. I promise you, with this level of control, there is absolutely no way that you will develop long-term complications from high blood sugar. Your blood sugar would have to sit at numbers double what yours have been reaching and stay there for weeks or months on end in order for you to even be considered a candidate for long term problems related to high blood sugar." Really? "Yes, really." She said it with a laugh that didn't make me feel silly, but instead made me feel loved.

"But what about the lows?" I asked, hoping for the same answer.

Dr. Peters thought for a moment and then said calmly, "Alex - there are patients with *poor control* who experience severe hypoglycemia on a daily basis so severe that they are left unconscious. If that were to happen to you, if you went so low that you were left unconscious for an extended period of time, multiple days in a week, then you might be causing some damage. But this has never happened to you. You have not caused physical damage to your brain. What you are doing is being incredibly hard on yourself. I can see that's the kind of person you are and that's how you've gotten to where you are today, but I want you to listen to me when I say that you don't have to be hard on yourself when it comes to diabetes. You're doing so well; better than most patients I see. You just need to get out of your own way, trust in the methods in place, and for heaven's sake stop stacking insulin because you really do not need to."

She said that it was incredibly rare to see a type 1 patient with an A1C as low as mine, that it was outstanding. She said it's not uncommon for type 1's to become disillusioned by the notion of perfection. She encouraged me to re-frame the way I thought about my A1C, suggested I look at my current number as almost perfect, and to not be afraid of raising my number just a little, to a high 5 mmol/L (90 mg/dl) or a low 6 mmol/L (108 mg/dl). She said doing so would, in fact, be perfect, and meant I would experience less lows and live a happier life.

We wrapped up the consultation with a hug, and a promise from me to feel pride as opposed to shame and to think before I pulled out the pen. I promised to let the insulin do its job, to work towards a slightly higher A1C upon my next visit and, most of all, stop being so hard on myself.

While driving home I felt warmer, lighter, more reassured. With all the windows wound down, a heavenly breeze washed over me as I thought about Anne, about how safe she made me feel, and how easily I felt I could talk to her. How effortlessly she got through to me, how undeniably intelligent she was yet entirely human. It felt so personal, so real.

After I saw Anne, I had to acknowledge that it wasn't the first time I heard a lot of what she said, however. I'd received very similar advice from various doctors, advice that I had been quick to dismiss and tuck away in the back corners of my mind. I only heard what I wanted to hear and disregarded the rest. I wondered why that was. I wondered if I had really tried to seek someone out, if I'd allowed myself to be vulnerable enough to trust someone, would I have found someone as perfect as Anne? Would I only find help once I really decided that I wanted some? Had I unknowingly bypassed opportunities to be helped in the past because I wasn't emotionally ready to accept that I needed it? Was it about trusting myself? Was it about trusting others? Or was this just fate?

28

HOW 'BOUT <u>NOW</u> BRO?

James and I moved in together somewhere around this time. I had my best friend by my side during the good days as well as the not-so-good ones. I'd also wanted a dog for us as long as I could remember. It took James a minute to come around to the idea, but one afternoon he sat me down and told me he thought it was time and that we should get one. He said a tongue flapping, floppy-eared friend would be a welcomed companion and a support to me on those days I felt like no one understood. We named her Billie the Boo, or Inspector Bilbo 'Popcorn' Baggins. She's a mini Australian Shepherd with a wonky stance, paws that smell like popcorn, moderate gastrointestinal issues, and the ability to turn any sadness or despair (diabetes-related or not) into a thing of the past with a lick of the face and a wiggle of her bubble butt. Mum came to visit, as she does every year, like a hurricane of sunshine and chicken soup, face masks and Australian TV show reruns. It was a rejuvenating distraction, since at that time we all nervously waited to hear whether or not *The Royals* had been picked up for a fifth season.

After seeing Dr. Peters, I tried so hard to rewire my brain, to strangle the angsty devil on my shoulder whenever its breathy monster-sounding-whispers nagged with opinionated judgement. *"Aaaaalex...your sugar is a little hiiiiigh! Better double up on insulin just in caaassseeee,"* said the devil. I kept this to myself, like usual, having been on this train for five years now. I was so fortunate for the Dex, for Dr. Peters, to be able to afford health insurance, for the bubble of perfection that is my life and I wanted more than anything to believe *my own story*, the story I'd told the people I loved. The one about how I was doing so much better, and how I really knew *this time* that I didn't need to correct anymore. The one about how I truly believed that *my control* was good enough.

I didn't though. I still didn't. I was addicted to this false sense of control and to a very warped perception of perfection. I felt ashamed for sneaking off into other rooms and giving myself shots while no one was looking, for failing to engage properly in normal conversation until I'd figured out a way to excuse myself and correct a number I believed required correction. I felt gross, but it was impossible for me to relax until I knew I was "taking control," and doing something to help me get back to the perfect straight line on the Dex. I hated myself for lying to my family who were understandably concerned and only wanted the best for me. My family, who weren't as oblivious to my lies as I pretended they were, but who were understandably running out of strategies to help me.

Dolled up and ready to hit the town, Mum, James and I barricaded Inspector Baggins into the kitchen. We watched her attempt to jump with her pee-wee legs over the makeshift fence enough times for us to almost put a rain check on the evening. Eventually we decided to toughen up, block out the heartbreaking, "don't leave me" cries and hit the road. We were off to see *Top Gun Live*. It was an interactive extravaganza paying tribute to Top Gun and other memorable Tom Cruise movie characters at a grungy theatre in Silver Lake. I was pumped for it regardless of the fact that I had absolutely no interest in *Top Gun* or Tom Cruise in general.

We arrived with time to spare for a welcomed preprandial in the form of some cheap liquor in a plastic cup. We observed the enthusiasm of the audience as they arrived, one by one, dressed as their favorite Tom Cruise characters and ready for a wild evening of retro-kitsch entertainment. While smiling at an enthusiastic James and cringing slightly in furtive glances to a less enthusiastic Mum, we were stopped by a man selling waterproof ponchos. On our way into the theatre, he informed us that there would be flying liquids incorporated into the show which, *naturally*, I was thrilled about. "Keep an open mind, Alex. Don't make James feel bad for bringing us here." Fuck yeah!!! Ponchos! Hit me! I love getting wet! (sigh) Mum! You look so cute in a poncho!

We got amongst it because why the fuck not. I grabbed a few last-minute drinks before the show started, took a few poncho selfies with Mum and actually yelled a bit during the pre-show festivities (everyone else was!). If you can't beat em,' join em' I say.

The show kicked off. There were many inside jokes that obviously Mum and I were not in on, but I had to give it to them. There were Nerf missiles zip-lining through the crowd, audience fueled paper plane battles, multiple karaoke singalong opportunities and dance-offs involving lucky members of the audience. It was cute as fuck actually. These nerds were so stoked it made me kinda stoked. I had my two favorite people sitting next to me and they both had huge smiles on their faces, which was the only thing that mattered. Except for my blood sugar, that mattered, it always did, even when I wished it wouldn't. During intermission, Mum popped off to the loo, James to the bar, and I stayed in my seat. I lifted my poncho and gave myself a few units, which made me feel guilty as I always did when sneaking insulin. But I'd been sitting at about a 9 mmol/L (162 mg/dl) since we left Inspector Baggins in the kitchen and I figured there must have been more sugar than I thought in the takeaway curry we had before we left. I had some glucose with me; I made sure of that. I'd check again before the show was over. Dex would keep me in the loop.

Slightly wet and a little tipsy as the show came to a roaring finish, it was my turn to go to the loo before we headed back home. My blood sugar was about the same as it was at intermission. It had been about an hour and a half since my last dose, and I knew we were going to have snacks when we got home. I figured another 2 units would bring the stubborn reading of 9 mmol/L (162 mg/dl) down to something that would accommodate my involvement in the post-show snacks.

Billie "the Boo" had developed an adorable tradition by this point. Whenever we arrived home and released her from her little caged area, she ran outside and down the steps to the gate, then ran up and down about six times more before she felt confident that everyone who arrived made it inside the house. We changed into track pants, lit the candles in the living room, put together a cheese board, and poured ourselves a nightcap.

I guess I forgot that I'd already given myself insulin in preparation for the snacks or maybe I decided that the dose I took wasn't enough. It had gotten me down to a 7 mmol/L (126 mg/dl), but I had a feeling that my previous shot wasn't going to take me down any further, as the arrow on the Dex was going across, rather than down. Maybe I just wasn't thinking at all but, yeah, I took some more, out in the open this time. I didn't feel the need to hide this shot, since we were about to eat, and Mum and James weren't aware of the two shots I took at the theatre.

I stood there in the kitchen and started to feel woozy. At first, I thought it was the alcohol that suddenly hit me like a freight train, but alcohol doesn't usually work like that. My heart rate sped up, as though activated via switch. My knees were weak and struggled to hold me up. All the symptoms of low blood sugar hit me at once, like, a leaf-blower blasting through my internal organs, leaving me weightless, like a wobbly feather. It felt like my soul was leaving my body at a rapid pace. The Dex still said I was fine, but I knew I'd blown it and I needed Glen.

"GLEN, GLEN," I started yelling at the top of my lungs, while slapping myself in the face and breathing rapidly.

"Where is your *glucose*, Alex?" said James frantically as he ran to the bedroom in search of the tablets.

Giving up on Glen, I headed to the living room, where I faintly recalled leaving a bottle of glucose tablets. I didn't care if I was high anymore, I'd eat the whole bottle. Just give me enough time to eat these things, I won't do it again (Do you believe me? I wouldn't).

"What's going on Al?!" said Mum with a look on her face that I'll never forget.

Leaning against an armchair, I desperately chewed as many of the hard chalky tablets as I could, but my jaw had started moving in slow motion, in-step with the rest of my body. I was panicking like I never had before.

"HELP HELP HELP" was what I remembered yelling as the insulin continued to plague my entire system and shut it down, what felt like, one organ at a time. Losing the fight to stay upright, I laid down on the floor. Mum tried to get me to chew the glucose tablets, but I couldn't do it.

You know when you're stuck in the middle of a really bad dream? It's one of those dreams that you know is a dream and the part of you that knows this, no matter how small, fights ferociously to wake up and halt the wicked narrative before you fall off the cliff? But you know deep down inside that, in order to break free, you'll have to fall? It felt a lot like that. Then, everything went black.

It wasn't until writing this section of the story that I actually asked Mum and James what it was like for them, once I had left them alone (back on earth), to clean up my mess. There was a big, dark gap in my memory, you see, between the cliff edge I fell from and the sharp jab of a glucagon pen that jolted me back to life as though I'd been shot with adrenaline. (A glycogen pen is used in emergencies for T1 patients who have fallen unconscious).

Mum always went on about the glucagon pen. She was fastidious and made sure I had one with me at all times, which I thought was an overreaction; Mum just being Mum. I told James he would never have to use it, and I honestly believed that. I believed a lot of incorrect things before that night.

After my eyes rolled to the back of my head, James and Mum said I started making rapid sucking noises and they were concerned I was going to have a fit.

It's very hard to write this, and it's very difficult to imagine how scared I must have made them. My Mum and my boyfriend, desperately trying to keep me alive. Two people who loved me unconditionally, regardless of the fact that I repeatedly ignored the best advice given by them and all my successive doctors.

James ran and retrieved the glucagon pen, then stood over my limp body as he figured out how to get the liquid glucose out of the vial and into the syringe. He wasn't totally sure where he was supposed to administer the shot so he pulled down my pants, aimed the needle to the top of my thigh and turned to Mum with a look that said "is this right?!" Mum gave him the go ahead, "Yes, do it. That looks right." In went the needle, then... they waited for it to work, not knowing for sure that it would. From James' retelling of the moment, that waiting period felt more like a week than the two or three tense minutes it actually took for me to wake up again. When my eyes eventually opened, I started violently throwing up, and asking what happened.

Breathing in the smell of my Mum, I laid tightly wrapped in her arms. I felt the cool sensation of her soft hands stroking my forehead, the beating drum of her heart pulsated through my back. All I could think about was how grateful I was for Mum and James, how had I been alone and left in that state, I could have died. I thought about how imperative it was for me to finally accept that I would never have the same blood sugar levels as people without my condition. I was ready to make peace with that. I never ever wanted this to happen again and knew that the only way to make sure it didn't was to get out of my own way, to accept imperfection.

Perfection is an illusion, it's not real; it's fabricated bullshit. It sounds fucked up, but I was grateful for what happened that night. I had to fall off the cliff in order to break free.

29

RISE 'N SHINE

Mum was set to head back home the next morning, but postponed her flight for a couple of days since James had to leave for a job out of state. I told her I'd be fine, but I was so grateful that she stayed. I emailed Dr. Peters, shamefully filled her in, and asked if there was anything I needed to do as this had obviously never happened before.

"You should be fine, but rest today and be careful as you will be more at risk of going low. That's a bad way to learn a lesson," she said sympathetically, yet sternly.

She continued, saying "Please refill your glucagon pen NOW, and please remember to listen to me in future!"

Message received, loud and clear.

Mum and I spent the day on the couch, cuddling, and watching *Friends*. She was gentle with me, as she always is, even though I would have understood completely had she not been. I told her how sorry I was, over and over, because I was - I was *so sorry* for lying to her. Mum told me it's impossible to be honest with others when you're not being honest with yourself. It's funny how life works sometimes isn't it? After an entire year of being apart, it wasn't until the two weeks Mum had come to visit that I finally hit rock bottom. I wondered if maybe Mum being there was part of the reason I was finally able to see the light as brightly as I did, to love myself again, to see myself as she does.

I tried really hard to keep the tears to a minimum while seeing Mum off at the airport. I've never been very good at that though, and the hardest part of living overseas has and will always be saying goodbye.

It's such an eerie, unnatural feeling, holding your loved ones in your arms so tightly before releasing them, watching them walk away and then continuing on your own, without them, not knowing how long it will be until you see them, smell them, touch them again. I have no idea what I did to deserve the love she makes me feel, my heart bursts at every thought of her.

So it was just Bill and I for a while. Man and dog. Inspector and space cadet. We spent the next week engaged in voiceless conversations, sitting quietly, listening to birds, walking aimlessly around the neighborhood, lost completely in our own complex universes. Billie teaches me valuable lessons every day about the power of the present, the infinite wonder that fills a single moment and the inner peace that comes with acceptance. Let me just pause here for a minute to let you know that by no means did I return home from my trip to the airport, sit down and make an executive decision to dedicate my week of solitude to active self reflection. It just kind of happened organically, on its own. Like it was going to happen whether I liked it or not. The time for rationality and humility had finally arrived.

Self-reflection is something I hadn't done a lot of over the past five years and it's the only real process by which you grow your understanding of who you are, what your values are, why you think and act the way you do. When the world is moving at a million miles an hour, it's hard to find your center, and to see things for what they really are. It's easy to get lost in the race, focusing only on what's happening next. Constantly pushing yourself like I was can make it very difficult to prioritize the sort of self-analysis that can bring your life into alignment with what you truly wish it to be.

I thought a lot about pride. How pride in oneself is absolutely necessary for some things, but that being *too proud* can hold you back from seeing reality and can cause you to make some serious mistakes. Like the old line in Proverbs that says, "pride goeth before destruction, and a haughty spirit before a fall."[9] It wasn't until that night that I actually accepted I had type 1 diabetes. I was too proud to really accept it in my heart of hearts until then. I didn't want to let it take over my life or for it to define me. So I fought against it. I fought doctors, technology, and the diabetes community. I fought any opinion that wasn't my own. I fought until I couldn't anymore to prove to myself that I was stronger than this condition, that I knew better, and that I had the power to defeat it on my own.

Looking back, it's become very clear that with every moment I managed to put my pride aside and just *listen and obey*, I saw improvement and felt less alone. The truth is that it takes courage to put your hand up and ask for help. It took me a while to realize that seeking help from others doesn't make us any less strong. It does the opposite. It makes us brave, equipped and powerful.

9   *1611, King James Version of the Bible, Book of Proverbs, 16:18*

I'd love more than anything to be able to tell you that I never had a bad hypo again after that night and be able to wrap this bitch up with an elaborate thesis full of all the type 1 diabetes secrets to success. I'd love to tell you that your doctor holds the holy grail, and that there is a specific method we with type 1 should follow so that we can all have smooth sailing and no more bad days if we just stick to the script. But I can't do that.

Our biological complexities are constantly changing based on so many different things that are often out of our physical control. Learning that doing your best *is enough*, in my opinion, is the most valuable lesson we can learn. Nobody has complete control over their bodies, because each individual body is a never-ending universe, no two humans are exactly the same. That's why many times even a doctor won't know what's going on with you because it's just not as simple as we want to believe it is.

So I started writing this story about a year ago. I didn't really know what the exact point of it would be, where I'd begin or how it would end. I just knew that I had a strong desire to share my experience. Being diagnosed with type 1 was the most random, bizarre thing that has ever happened to me (and I've had a few strange experiences you might agree). While it made a lot of my day-to-day life exponentially more difficult, it also changed me for the better. While I hated it, fought, and lost to it for the better part of five years, I'd also been utterly fascinated by it.

I'd never had an excuse to really dive inside the biological complexities of my body, to play games with it, test it, experiment and really learn about it. I mean, *think about it*. We are born in these magnificent, entirely unique complex organic machines. We grow in these bodies inside our mothers wombs, like a seed that turns into a flower. We talk, we think, we eat. We go to the doctor when we get sick, or we might take a painkiller when we get a head-ache. We attempt to stop the dark red liquid from pour-ing out of our skin by covering it with a plaster. We ice our ankles when they ache and drink warm milk when we can't sleep. We feel happy after we exercise and get some endorphins pumping. Our limbs move. We jump, dance, swim, we feel cold, sad, angry, euphoric. We do and feel all these incredible mind-blowing things in these mysterious bodies without even really knowing how. It's all so automatic, so normal, so easy. We don't even have to think about it.

But then something happens, something under the skin that we weren't expecting, something we can't see. You might have heard of something called a pancreas, if you were listening in school (I wasn't). The word is slightly familiar, but what does it do? You never had to know before. Before, it was just *there*, squashed together amongst all the other organs whose names you may or may not have remembered either. The pancreas deliv-ers insulin, they say. Insulin. What the shit is insulin? Oh, fairly important, you say? Then, only because you absolutely have to know, you find out that insulin is the substance responsible for making sure the food you eat actually nourishes your body. Then you read on with horror, as you discover that without it, there's no point to the food whatsoever. The food won't work, and you wouldn't survive without it. Fuck, OK then. So my pan-creas has decided to stop working and the pancreas is super important. Well, *bloody hell*. What a fucking night-mare. How come it stopped working? You might ask. Well we aren't entirely sure, they say. Something about "autoimmune,"or a number of other equally long and alien-sounding words. Well I've heard of that, couldn't tell you what it means though. Right, so my body has attacked itself. Shit. That doesn't sound good at all.

You'll be fine though, they say. You can live with it. One hundred years ago, it would have been a death sentence, but they've figured out a way to artificially replicate the insulin. It's complicated though, since you can't just inject it in the morning and hope it'll help you when you need it. You have to time it perfectly. You have to measure how much gets into your body, and you have to be prepared all the time for everything to be wrong, even if you've done it a million times before. Jeez. Right, OK. So how do I do that? Well. There are a million different opinions on how best you can do that, but at the end of the day, it's different for everybody. Huh? You've got to be joking. So there's not a manual? Something I can rope-learn? A system, perhaps? One that if followed correctly, everything will run smoothly? Well, no, sadly. No, there's not. Not exactly. You'll have to figure the bulk of it out on your own.

Type 1 diabetes is not terminal. How absolutely blessed are we, realistically, to be alive in this time, where we have some sort of an ability to choose how this condition affects our lives? Imagine feeling slightly unwell, sitting down in a doctor's office and being told that whatever was making us feel off-color will kill us, and that we might live a few more months or even years. But that eventually, we would die, and that there is nothing that can be done. Imagine not having a choice as to whether you live or die. Imagine getting that news on a Friday afternoon when you went in for a check up, assuming you'd be prescribed something that, within a couple of weeks, would leave you feeling brand new, ready to get back to the rest of your life.

Let's take a quick spin through the history of diabetes for a minute, just to get a bit of perspective in terms of just how incredibly fortunate we are.

Before the discovery of insulin, just ninety-eight years ago, a couple of years before my grandma was born, diabetes was a fatal disease. The only therapy available was the starvation diet, which pretty much speaks for itself. An extremely restricted diet based on proteins and fat nutrients. A diet which, when followed to the letter, might extend a patient's life expectancy by a measly year or two. But, typically, adults lived under two years post-diagnosis, while children rarely lived longer than one. Some life, huh? Two years of suffering starvation and painful, torturous, heartbreak all while anticipating the gradual inevitable shut down of your entire body.

This wasn't that long ago.

There was no such thing as a glucose monitor back then either, nothing of the sort. They didn't know how to test blood for glucose levels until the 1960s, and that's just sixty years ago! They used to use eight drops of urine, which were then mixed in a *test tube* with some kind of solution named Benedict, and then put into boiling water for five minutes. I mean, COME ON. Can you imagine having to conduct a legitimate science experiment every single time you wanted to check your blood sugar? With no real clue as to whether they were even going to be accurate?

When they finally developed test strips for testing drops of blood for glucose, the first iteration certainly wasn't an on-the-go job either. You'd place a drop of blood on a paper strip for a minute, wash it off, and then compare the color shades on a chart, which would provide a rough indication of glucose levels. Essentially, the best medical solution available was a colour-by-numbers game where each patient's interpretation of different shades of red needed to be spot-on identical - which was obviously impossible - or the reading would likely be inaccurate.

The first ever portable glucose monitor arrived about fifteen years later in the late 1970s, and is fondly remembered as the guillotine. Sorry - hold up a minute. The GUILLOTINE? In a nutshell, this old boy had the body of a retractable tape measure with three main sections that all had different jobs. There was a little plastic circle-platform-thing poking out the bottom; that's where your finger would go. About six inches above was an angled, spring-loaded lever holding the lancet, an alarmingly large spiky thingy, which would need to be cocked back like a rifle. From here you'd hold your breath and do everything you could to keep the finger on the platform as you pressed the trigger and the lever came careening down, slamming the lancet into your poor little finger tip. Sounds dreamy, *right?* It was leaps and bounds from the old test tubes and benedict solution, but I'd imagine it was ferociously painful. I don't think I'd bring the guillotine to brunch with the girls. At the same time, if I only had test tubes to go on, I'd order as many guillotines as I could get my hands on.

I mean, I really could go on and on, but this isn't a history book. The point is 100 years ago, those with type 1 had a similar prognosis to those with cancer. People living with type 1 up to 50 years ago had a better shot at a relatively long life, but not without extreme difficulty. Today, thanks to decades of trial and error, scientific experiment, unwavering persistence, and the countless fatalities of type 1 patients before us, we have free online education, advanced technology, and forever-improving medications that allow us the freedom to make a choice. We can decide at which degree we want this condition to affect our health. You can simply choose to leave it, you can check willy nilly, you can eat all the crap food that you like. You can even play the poor little match girl out in the snow and use your condition as an excuse to get everyone to feel sorry for you. You can do that! IT'S YOUR CHOICE! Your other option, however, and the one I highly recommend, is to consider how much worse it could be, truly, even just 50 years ago. Afterwards, you do everything in your power to figure out exactly what you need to do to live the *longest, healthiest, and BEST* life there is; the one that will allow you to fight for your dreams.

It's easy to be beaten down by hardship, but through the power of gratitude, it can be overcome. A while back I started meditating and exploring mindfulness as an extra treatment for the anxiety over my condition. I don't do it as much as I'd like to, but through meditation I have learned that the act of gratitude has the ability to eradicate sadness, change the way we think and the way we see the world. This notion has stayed with me every day since I first learned it; because it worked and still works. It works every time. One day I was feeling unhappy, as at times we all do, plagued with ugly thoughts of despair. I was inspired to close my eyes and make an internal list of all the things I am grateful for. By the time I got to number two, I felt a noticeable change in my energy. My heart rate slowed and I felt lighter. As soon I started to focus on the positives, I was able to notice that there were so many more positives than I previously considered, which naturally led to a feeling of appreciation. I no longer felt helpless and sad, instead I felt inspired, thankful and calm. Not only do the practice of mindfulness and relaxation techniques have the power to reframe our perspective, they also have the ability to improve our physical health. This goes for everyone, but in terms of type 1 diabetes, stress creates insulin resistance - causing high blood sugar. To put it bluntly: calm mind = body happy. Stressed mind = body angry. It makes a lot of sense when you really think about it - so I'd highly recommend making time to prioritize daily moments of Zen. It really helps me, anyway.

You can choose to let this thing beat you, or you can choose to see the bigger picture. If you're reading this from a first world country, try to remember that even on the really tough days, there are many out there dealing with the same condition and everyone might not be able to afford the life-saving technology that this infuriatingly complex disease requires you to keep buying to stay alive. There are thousands of children in developing countries whose health services still don't have the facilities to test blood sugar. This leaves many sufferers unaware as to why they are so ill. There are children who walk four hours to get the bus to the hospital for their medication. They do this every day because insulin needs to be refrigerated, and they can't afford refrigerators. They can't take it home with them, otherwise it would spoil. I learned all of this through the International Diabetes Federation's Life for a Child program. It's a charity I support that provides care, education, life-saving medicines and support to children with diabetes in the developing world. We can let our help towards others, help us. We can let our own misfortune be someone else's good fortune. What better feeling is there than knowing our hard work, determination and belief in something could actually help others? We have the power to do this. To me, this is the greatest gift.

We can lift ourselves up and strengthen our mission as individuals by standing together, sharing our knowledge and fighting for a world whereby everyone with type 1 diabetes, no matter where they live, has everything they need to survive and achieve their dreams. I am aware of my financial privilege, meaning that I can afford to pay the insanely high premiums charged by the perversely unjust healthcare system in America, but many cannot. Worldwide, there are people with type 1 diabetes who are being economically suffocated, and in some cases *dying*, because they can't afford the drugs that keep them alive from day to day. There are initiatives like T1International, who, with our help, continue to fight the big pharmaceutical and insurance companies that keep treatments out of the hands of those that need them and only into the hands of those who can pay their prices. Every human, child or adult, regardless of where they are, should have access to everything they need to stay alive and follow their dreams. It's clear that the type 1 diabetic community's passionate engagement and collaboration has made a real difference on these fronts. Together we can ensure that it continues to do so.

Meanwhile, I'm still working through the personal journey every day. It doesn't stop. There's no end point where I've completed all the levels. I'm still learning, improving, and persevering. However, I now have an A1C of 5.5 (bang on), my hypoglycemic frequency has decreased by 85% (waaaay less hypos) and I'm the healthiest I have ever been due to the choices I've made and the help I've received. Here's the real *kicker*: I feel stronger now than I ever did before I was diagnosed because this disease has helped me really *know and improve* myself biologically and as a human being in general.

The beauty of making the decision to *figure out what's right for you* is that, once you find it, no matter how long it takes, you get to keep that information and *it's yours*. It's so good for you! It's laser focusing on how to take care of *you*! Whatever it is that's making you feel like this thing is beating you, try to remember that you really are in the drivers seat. It's not terminal and there *are* ways to make it better. Thanks to advances in medical technology, *you* decide the direction it goes. When you fall down, try again and don't give up just because it's hard, even if it feels like you're getting nowhere. Just. Keep. Trying. Use your struggles to fuel your fire.

When you have bad days, and you will, lean on your friends and reach out for help. Let others remind you of how strong you are when you're struggling to see it for yourself. It's hard. The other day, after I'd finished typing out the post-Top Gun-living-room-hypo story, I went for a hike with James and Inspector Baggins to celebrate the fact that I'd almost completed the first draft of whatever it was I'd been writing for the last year (the book you are reading right now!). The sun was amber in the Hollywood Hills and we were a bit scared of snakes as the flora was thicker than usual. But the wind was in my hair and I felt like a million bucks. Once we had gotten about halfway down the trail, I started to feel like I was going to pass out. I had *one measly* tube of glucose gel with me, so I downed it quickly in a knee-jerk reaction. As the glucose hit the back of my throat, I remembered I'd given myself insulin back at home and had forgotten to have a snack before we left for the hike. This was quite literally minutes after working on a book that warned against this specific kind of mistake. We were about an eight minute uphill run from where the car was parked, but I was dropping rapidly, so James ran back to the car to get more glucose. I kept walking and steadied myself with the pull of Billie's leash until I had to sit down. I was dangerously low, again. It was the worst hypo I'd had in months. I felt like a fraud and I couldn't write for a few days. I couldn't write until I was reminded by the people that I love that it's not about the mistakes we make, it's about the way we handle our mistakes, what we decide to take from them, and how we choose to move forward.

30

Come fly with me

It was my first day of year seven. High school, as they call it in Australia. I told Mum that I didn't want her to come in with me and that she could just drop me at the gate. I was 13, after all. This would be the 4th and, hopefully last time I was the new kid at school. I'd never been very good at following maps, but persevered with vigor to locate my assigned home room via the crumpled piece of paper they'd given me during orientation. I wound my way through the maze of hallways, taking care to dodge the melee of students as they made their way into their various classrooms. It became apparent that everybody seemed to know where they were going, except for me. Great. Not only was I the new kid, I was the *late* new kid.

I arrived at classroom *A4* about 15 minutes after everybody else did. I received the standard "This is Alex, she's new, let's make her feel welcome" introduction from my teacher. I stood there with my backpack still on, a layer of sweat dripping down my forehead and a frog in my throat. The faces of twenty or so students looked me up and down, drinking in every detail.

"Who's got a spare seat next to them for Alex?" The teacher said to the sea of bobbing pony tails. A few hands kind of half went up during this excruciating moment of silence, before a tall, tanned girl in the back corner stood up and waved me over.

"You can sit next to me!" She said.

Her name was Benedicte. She was beautiful, confident, and French. Everybody knew her and, from that day on, she was my best friend. Everything I did for the first time, I did with Benedicte. I wasn't cool before I knew Benedicte. She made me cool, by association. It was a tremendous gift to bestow. We kissed boys for the first time on the same night. We drank alcohol together for the first time and we hid under our duvets and told each other when we first got our periods. We even ran away to each other's houses when our parents were splitting up. She was Ariel the mermaid and I was her adoring Flounder, swimming along behind her, following her every move.

When school ended, we stayed in touch while going separate ways. It's one of those friendships that you know in your heart will always remain. A year could go by and nothing will have changed, more like family than friendship.

A month or so ago (or about 10 pages back, for those reading along), I woke up with a faint instinct that something peculiar was on the horizon. You know those mornings, when you open your eyes and stare at the ceiling in utter stillness and silence? One by one, the individual components of your system boot up, not unlike a baby dinosaur, cracking its way out of its shell, one teensy push at a time. I stood in my undies, having a stretch, as I normally do each morning. Then I flicked on the kettle and checked my messages. There was one from Benedicte; we'd spoken just a few days prior. She'd sent me photos from the beach, just checking in, as mates do. But this morning, her message was to tell me that she had, in fact, just been diagnosed with type 1 diabetes.

After calling six times and sending 23 text messages, all the while fully aware it would be a good five hours until she would be awake back home in Sydney, I paced around the house. I was charged up like a Tesla, checking the Australian clock every 20 minutes until finally I heard from her.

"*Hey bro*, I'm up. Just doing these bloody *blood things* that are through the roof,' she texted, foggily. "I have no idea what I'm doing."

"Let me help," I said. "Can we speak? Facetime? Or regular?"

As soon as my buddy's face appeared on the screen of my phone, all the talking points I had judiciously prepared in my mind dissipated in an oozy moment of nostalgic familiarity. We just stared at each other for a bit, making *WTF?* faces, before agreeing that now we really were *connected for life*.

"*Mate*. What the fuck? Are you ok? What can I do? I don't even know where to begin?"

She was wearing her pajamas, gingerly holding an insulin pen as she attempted to bring me up to speed.

"Oh, *you know*, I was just feeling like *absolute shit* for the past three weeks. I couldn't even get out of bed. I thought I had the bloody coronavirus, but my symptoms were everything but respiratory. So I told the doctor I wanted to be tested for everything, like literally everything they got."

She said this while attempting to attach the needle to the end of the pen.

"It just fucking hurts, doesn't it? Like, how do you deal with the pain of this shit *every day*?"

"Hold on a sec, man, let me get mine. I'll show you a little trick."

I propped the phone up on the table and shimmied my right butt cheek a little, so it was visible on the screen. Then, I grabbed a fatty bit of skin and pushed it together with my left hand.

"See, you wanna squeeze it together with your thumb and your index finger, so it forms a little cushiony lump. Hold it there, and make sure you've clicked the dosage to the right amount, and then swiftly jab it directly into the skin between your fingers."

"Ahhhh OK. That makes sense. And so you do it in your butt, do you? I've been doing it in my stomach and it fucking hurts."

I laid down on the bed so that I could do a sweeping shot of all my injection sites. I told her that it's important to rotate the places you inject your insulin, since jabbing in the same spot every time will cause fatty tissue to build up, which obviously we don't have time for.

Then we just shot the shit for a while. There was so much I wanted to say, but I was conscious that I didn't want to overwhelm her so early on in her diagnosis. I vividly remembered what it was like to be where she was, emotionally blown-over, while holding onto the hope that maybe this was just a dream, and that *just maybe* they had got it wrong.

"So I've lost about 5kg, which is about the only good thing that's come out of this whole thing," said Benedicte. "But the doctor told me that once I started using insulin, it would all come back on, so that's fucking great." It was all a bit like deja vu.

"You're not gonna get fat man, I promise you. Your body is just all over the place right now. Everything will settle down and you'll be just as stunning as you are right now."

We talked about alcohol. It was one of the first things I thought about too. I mean it's hard not to. We're Australian, after all. I told her about what I'd learned: that beer, white wine and sugary cocktails weren't really an option for us anymore, but that the inimitable Don Draper drinks whiskey straight and we could too. In fact, it's kind of a reverse benefit, because it makes one look much classier. I also relayed that if whiskey wasn't her preference, rosé, red wine and spirits in general were generally OK as well.

"It's all about trial and error man, you'll get the hang of it. It's gonna be a headache for a minute, but I'm here, 24/7. Any question you have is a question that, at some stage, I've wanted the answer too as well. Remember that!"

She told me that her doctor wanted her to eat carbs and that there should be a portion in every meal. This made my stomach do a quick backflip, but before vomiting my conflicting opinion about that little suggestion, I realized that I wasn't really in the position to tell her to do the opposite. We weren't the same person. I figured that telling her to stop eating carbs before she'd even properly wrapped her head around what was going on could lead to her having terrifying hypos, and that scared the shit out of me. She was going to have to figure that out on her own (which she did). I realized that as much as I wanted to help her in any way I could, I also had to be careful to focus mainly on listening and being there for her emotionally. I tried to offer advice if she asked for it, but remembered that all the things that made "Bene'" (pronounced 'Benny') *Bene*, would make her path different to mine.

Two people can be infatuated with one another. They can be as thick as thieves, or get along like Tom and Jerry, but at the end of the day Tom and Jerry aren't the same person. Bene's always followed the rules a bit more closely than I have. She respected authority a little more than I did. While she was always up for whatever stupid shit I had planned, she'd always make sure, after we were done, that we made it back to school on time. In year 12, I put my hand up for the "champagne breakfast" before school as soon as the suggestion was on the table. The 'champagne breakfast' turned out to be more like drinking four packs of vodka cruisers in the park adjacent to our school - while in full school uniforms - and I was promptly expelled along with a few other loveable delinquents. Bene had the foresight to sit that one out because she considered the consequences. She graduated with the rest of the class like the obedient student she was. She was also super pissed off with us for doing what we did, since it resulted in her having to go to prom without her stupid reckless friends.

She's not as quick to dismiss opinions based on how they make her feel emotionally, as I have been known to do. She's always been a planner, extremely organized, a bit of a worry wart, and overall a lot more grounded than I was. As the old saying goes "opposites attract."

So it's been about six weeks since Bene was diagnosed. We speak from time to time, and I think about her every day. It's been pretty bizarre, really. After traveling the better part of this road alone, finally getting to a place where I feel like I've got this thing under control and one of my best mates all the way on the other side of the world is taking her first steps towards the same destination, but via a different road.

I've had to learn how to walk the fine line between attempting to help Bene by using examples from my own experience and knowing that her solutions won't necessarily be the same as mine. I'm not sure if I told you about my Math class…but basically, it took place in a janitors closest with just three other "special" numerically challenged students like myself....and Bene was one of the other three. So, when she told me she'd been following the "nutritional guidelines" (which, in my experience, were a fucking hoax) and counting carbs (which never worked for me) to decipher her insulin ratio, but was still failing to see balanced numbers, I wasn't about to tell her to just wing it like I did. Despite both of us being shit at math, Bene's not like me. She doesn't just wing things, she follows the rules and using math as a method certainly takes her kind of patience. Just because it didn't work for me, doesn't mean it won't work for her.

I helped where I felt I could without confusing her. As an example, she went to dinner with some friends, a Thai restaurant (very big in Sydney), and felt confused as to what she might be able to order. So I had a look at the menu and told her that in my experience Thai as a whole was *pretty tricky*, since they like to use a lot of sugar in their cooking. Nevertheless, I circled the dishes I would have selected and simply reminded her that trying was the only real way to learn. That it might not feel like it now, but it will all start to make sense eventually.

Bene's doctor felt strongly about her potentially going on a plant-based diet, which to me, is absolutely batty, as there hasn't been a single vegan dining experience that I didn't end up regretting. A lot of what her doctor suggested left me baffled, but then I remembered that there has been plenty of advice given to me from doctors that I wished I would have listened to.

I can't tell my friend what to do; her path will be hers alone. But I do get to be there and remind her on hard days of the things I do know for certain. When she's burnt out, I can tell her she will figure this out, it just takes time, and that I'm the proof. I get to be the one to remind her of how strong she is and that finding the answers she seeks won't be an easy task, but that nothing truly worthwhile ever comes easy. That the only way to conquer this thing is to not let it conquer you.

If she asks me "Am I going to be OK?" I can say yes. I can even say, quite honestly, that she has a unique opportunity to be in better health than she ever was before, that she will be better than ok and she will never be alone. A few days after Bene was diagnosed, she wrote me a text I thought I'd share to tie a bow around this bad boy. She said "I love you. I feel so guilty that you had no one," to which my reply was: "My being alone was worth it, because now I get to be there for you."

ALEXANDRA PARK is an Australian actress, writer and producer. Park's career started with roles on some of Australia's most popular shows, including "Home and Away," "Packed to the Rafters" and "Elephant Princess." Weeks after moving to Los Angeles, Alex landed a leading role in Lionsgate's TV series, "The Royals," opposite Elizabeth Hurley and William Mosely, which she starred in for all four seasons. Alex can also be seen in the critically-acclaimed feature film, "Ben is Back," directed by Peter Hedges. Most recently, Park produced and starred in "Everyone is Doing Great," a crowd-funded comedy television series, which is now streaming in the U.S. on Hulu and all across the world on Paramount+. Balancing the ongoing demands of her career, while simultaneously juggling the ever-changing circumstances of type 1 diabetes, *Sugar High* is Alexandra's memoir and literary debut. Park currently resides in Los Angeles with her fiancé and a rambunctious miniature Australian shepherd, Billie.

Instagram | @AlexandraPark1

Manufactured by Amazon.ca
Bolton, ON

27560668R00166